WOMEN WRITE NOW

Other Anthologies by Something Or Other Publishing:

Midwest Road Trip Adventures
Copyright 2020

25 Servings of SOOP
Literary Journeys into Life, Meaning, and Love
Volume I
Copyright 2020

25 Servings of SOOP
Stories of Emotion, Contemplation, Laughter, and Imagination
Volume II
Copyright 2021

Passionately Striving in 'Why'
An Anthology of Women Who Persevere Mightily to Live Their Purpose
Copyright 2021

Winners
A Compilation of Award Winning Short Stories
Copyright 2022

All of the above may be ordered on Amazon or by visiting:
https://soopllc.com/product-category/books/anthologies/

WOMEN WRITE NOW

WOMEN IN TRAUMA

CURATED BY EDNA J. WHITE

ISBN: 978-1-954102-07-1

Library of Congress Control Number: 2022947415
Printed in the United States of America
First Printing: 2022

Curated by Edna J. White
Edited by Kate Johnston, Eileen Maddocks, Beth Rule
Cover design by Veronica Coello and Dragan Bilic
Interior design by Michael Grossman

Something Or Other Publishing LLC
Brooklyn, Wisconsin 53521
For general inquiries: Info@SOOPLLC.com
For bulk orders: Orders@SOOPLLC.com

CONTENTS

FOREWORD

Edna J. White

It feels strange for me to write these words after overcoming so many challenges to get to the point of publication. When I first was approached by SOOP to be a curator for this book, I was excited! However, I never dreamed how things would change in 2019, nor that we'd go through so many changes with the project itself.

When I was asked what I'd like to call the project, I came up with the title *Women Write Now*. I am awestruck by the powerful and courageous stories told within this book. The bravery of these women seemed to carry us through the difficulties we had to endure getting this project off the ground. Their stories needed to be told, and we got it done.

We have a great team.

Women Write Now is a collection of stories written by women about a time in their lives when they had been most in despair. These authors share a part of themselves that will serve as a beacon of hope to inspire others to recognize their own courage. We all have inner resources to help us through the dark, and these stories are a testament to how strong and brave we can be—even when things seem impossible.

This book is a powerful antidote to the toxic trauma that batter many of us. These beautiful stories can point us in a healthy direction that will not only help us heal but can positively impact future generations.

ONCE UPON A PINK BALLOON

Laura Harper

"Do you want a balloon?"

He was talking to me but his eyes were on my mom. We had gone to the Chevy dealership that day to fix a broken part on her brand-new car, the one my pap bought for her since she lost everything along with her nursing license for writing a fake prescription for Percocet. Now a strange man was looking at my mom, and I was looking at him and nodding because little girls like balloons and he knew that.

He guided us to the Secret Room in the back of the dealership where they stored bags of cheap balloons meant for adorning cheap cars and a big silver helium tank that seemed to tower over my nine-year-old head. He picked out a pink balloon because I'm a girl and girls like pink, then he filled it with helium while asking my mom if she was single.

She said she was. I thought of my dad.

He asked where she worked.

She said she was a nurse at Mercy Hospital. I thought about speaking up.

But then he was tying a string around the end of the balloon and handing it to me while he asked my mom for her number, which she gave him. I rubbed the textured string between my thumb and forefinger. I wanted to get away from this place that smelled like the floor wax at my school. I wanted to get away from this man who called my mom pretty and looked in my direction just long enough to tell her that I look just like her, even though I see the world through my dad's brown eyes.

—

His name was Dean.

He was one of nine children, the product of a bipolar schizophrenic father and a mother who received beatings from her husband and passed them on to her children. His parents kicked Dean and his siblings out of the house on their eighteenth birthdays, forcing them to find their own way as adults. Dean found refuge with a sympathetic aunt who kindly looked the other way when her nephew indulged in cocaine and alcohol.

Dean eventually collected so many DUIs that his driver's license was revoked with the condition that he could reinstate it if he paid a hefty fine and installed a breathalyzer in his car. To hear him tell it, that lit a fire under his ass and inspired him to quit the drinking and the drugs and get a job as a car salesman at the Chevy dealership where my mom had to take her car for repairs.

Apparently, he was so good at selling cars that his bosses kindly looked the other way when he would take customers for test drives without a valid driver's license.

—

My mom was a success story gone wrong.

She graduated from the Mercy Hospital School of Nursing, a prestigious program that accepted few and graduated fewer. To hear her tell it, she breezed through nursing school and earned herself a well-paying job right away, then married her longtime boyfriend and had a baby. Soon after the baby was born, she scored a dream job as a nursing supervisor, part-time of course, so she could focus on her daughter. She would always take that little girl to the mall and the nail salon, telling her that as soon as she was old enough, the two of them would go out for a Spa Day to get manicures and pedicures.

Somewhere along the way, she developed a taste for Vicodin after taking one to get rid of an especially stubborn migraine. Stealing the occasional pain pill from the med carts at work turned into stealing a prescription pad and attempting to have narcotics filled at the pharmacy. She succeeded once and failed the second time, leading to her arrest and the revocation of her nursing license. Soon after, her once happy marriage turned into a verbal battle-ground of mistrust and blame.

She lost her job and then lost her husband, since she also developed a taste for cheating.

The first time Dean broke up with my mom, he blamed it on me.

I was sitting in the backseat of the same red Cobalt that had needed repairs just a few weeks prior, with Dean behind the wheel, weaving in and out of traffic. We were on our way home from the zoo, a yearly occasion that I used to share with my parents, when I blurted out in quite the childlike fashion that I wished my mommy and daddy were still together.

Later that night, before swallowing a handful of anxiety medication, my mom made sure to tell me that Dean left her because he thought dating a woman with a child was too much baggage, especially one that clearly wanted her Real Dad. She then rolled over on our shared bed and went to sleep, and I watched her breathing to make sure it wouldn't stop. I was old enough to know that taking too much medicine was dangerous.

However, I was not old enough to know what "baggage" was. I worked my developing brain to find the connection between children and suitcases until I fell asleep.

A few days later, Dean decided that I was a manageable suitcase after all and took my mom back. He took her back the next time too, and the time after that, all the while making sure that my mom knew she was at fault each time.

The rhythm of their Light Switch Relationship became the rhythm of my life. When they were On Again, my mom would be a mother, laughing with me and singing songs in the car with the windows down and her dyed blonde hair dancing in the wind. When they were Off Again, my mom would be the child, and I had to make sure she ate and brushed her teeth and changed her clothes. Sometimes, I would skip school just to make sure I wouldn't have to come home and find her lifeless body beside an empty pill bottle. She wrote a lot of excuses to the school saying I was sick with the flu or the latest stomach bug, but the real sickness was in my head.

It did not take long for Dean to realize that I had an anxiety problem, and that my anxiety was largely centered on my mom. One day, he convinced her that it would be quite the funny prank for her to be laying on the couch when I came home from school and not respond when I tried to wake her up. As always, she did as she was told and stretched out face-down on the pillows, staying perfectly still and silent as I pushed and pulled and screamed her name. When I started to cry and grabbed the phone to call for help, Dean emerged from the bedroom, laughing.

With a smile, he told me that he killed her.

Only then did my mom sit up, and when my tears turned to anger, he called me crazy. He said anyone who cries without reason is crazy. From that day forward, he would label all of my anxiety episodes accordingly, until his voice played like a constant mantra in my head.

Crazy filled me up like a balloon, swelling until my head felt ready to burst.

—

Dean waited until my mom was fully addicted to him before he showed everything he was capable of. His common reasons for their

Biweekly Breakups were my mom lying to him about unspecified topics and cheating on him with unspecified people. I once tried to tell him that I was with my mom the whole time, alone in our tiny one-bedroom apartment, but he accused me of lying for her. In fact, he said I was too stupid to even sound convincing. He allowed my mom to be depressed for a few more days so that she could "learn her lesson," and when he took her back, he expressed how lucky she should consider herself that she found a man so forgiving.

Over time, he began to require that she present her phone so that he could read her texts and Facebook messages, which she always willingly did. He then told her that she was no longer allowed to work, so she quit her jobs and stayed home while he continued smooth-talking customers into buying cars outside of their budgets. When she needed money to put gas in her car, he would give her ten dollars at a time—just enough to make it to her parents' house and back home again. When he asked for something, she never denied his requests.

Many times, those requests involved having me make up excuses to ask my dad for more money beyond his five hundred dollars per month child support payments. While Dean watched, I called my dad and asked for twenty, fifty, or even a hundred dollars to go to the mall with friends I was never allowed to see or buy supplies for a nonexistent school project.

Each time my dad would agree, saying he would be over later that night or the next day to drop off the cash. I would fill with guilt as he handed me the money through his truck window, telling me that he was excited to spend time with me during our Wednesday evening and biweekly Friday through Sunday visits. I wanted to tell him everything that my mom and I were going through, but I couldn't. If I did, Dean would see that as betrayal. So I kept my mouth shut, to protect my mom.

I even kept my mouth shut when I learned that Dean had purchased two stamp bags of heroin from his neighbor, one for himself and one for my mom, just to try it once for fun. She agreed to it that one time, and the next time too, and the time after that. In fact, she agreed to it every single time for the next seven years.

———

Heroin addiction is unique in a lot of ways, but its standout feature is the way it makes users desperate. For Dean, it made him squander the impressive $22,000 balance in his bank account within just a few months. For my mom, it turned her into a thief, stealing my grandma's jewelry and my pap's brass trains to sell at pawn shops for quick cash.

I like to think that my mom would have never done these things without Dean whispering in her ear to take action if she really loved him, but her addiction raged just as badly as his. He often ordered her on drug runs to secure heroin from his two main dealers, and my mom would always bring me along because she was too scared to go alone, for fear of what these men might do to her. I vowed to do whatever I could to protect her.

When I was thirteen, Dean sent my mom to a new dealer, offering nothing but a warning that this guy had a tendency to be "shady." Once more, I tagged along with my mom. At the time, I was unaware that he would not let her leave until she tested the product in his spare bedroom. I also did not know that he had previously undergone investigation for accusations of child molestation.

I had no idea at all that he would tell me how beautiful I was with one hand on my back and the other on my thigh while my mom was getting high in the next room.

I kept my mouth shut and my eyes straight ahead. If I looked into his eyes, I would see the all-too-familiar pinpricks of a heroin addict where his pupils should be.

I could feel that balloon of anxiety rising in my stomach as I realized that this man was truly Crazy, the very thing I worked for years to convince myself that I wasn't despite Dean's voice echoing in my head.

———

Even then, it took another three years before I hit the Officially Had Enough milestone. I ran away from home when I was sixteen and started telling the True Stories to all the people I had told Fake Stories to in order to protect my mom and the addiction that consumed her. I could no longer sit there and watch her kill herself at least four times a day. It was making me Crazy.

I struggled to let go of my mom in a similar way to how she struggled to let go of Dean. She knew that he was bad for her. She knew that she was being manipulated, but her love ran so deeply that she convinced herself she could save him somehow, change him. Every time she promised not to answer his calls, she was defeated by the phony regret and unspoken apologies dripping from his voice.

For me, I felt an obligation to protect my mom, feeling that maybe, just maybe, I could love her enough for her to no longer depend on the poisoned love from Dean and her drug of choice. But abuse doesn't work that way, both in the sense of relationships and addiction. No matter how many times I tried to encourage her to take a walk or a drive with me and talk about what she was going through, it never seemed to be enough. I never seemed to be enough.

I wish I could say that my mom eventually found the strength to leave Dean on her own, but one day their Light Switch Relationship turned off and never turned back on again. Simply put, he just never called back. I later learned that Dean checked himself into a rehab facility and had most people believing that he was on the road to recovery when they found his lifeless body in a motel room next to an empty bottle of pills.

After running away from home and starting life over with my dad, it took over three months for me to get back on speaking terms with my mom. Within a year, her dealer, the same one accused of child molestation, was arrested for murdering his girlfriend, cutting off the only connection she had to her precious drug of choice.

From that moment forward, she liked to say that she never had a heroin problem in the first place. She said she just liked the way it made her feel, and she could have stopped using any time she wanted. Sometimes, she feels bad about what she put me through, smothering me with apologies and telling me how grateful she is to have such a caring, understanding daughter. Most of the time, she continues to assume the mind of an addict convinced that the world did her wrong, and I am just one more thing put on this earth as an obstacle.

For most of my life, I saw myself as a balloon, with my mom holding the string. I was bound to her, an Adolescent Protector, but she was bound to Dean and the drug he presented to her. For most of my life, I felt that I could never become more than what she was.

But then, one day, my string snapped. Whether it was my own will or the natural progression of time that caused it, I can't really say. I found myself somewhere new, somewhere safe inside my own head, free from Crazy. Free from control.

Free from me.

~ ~

Laura was born and raised in Pittsburgh, Pennsylvania, and has used writing as a form of escapism for as long as she can remember. She received a business degree from Point Park University with a minor in creative writing, and it was there where she met a professor who helped foster her love of Creative Nonfiction and gave her the freedom to embrace her story and grow as a writer. Now, Laura shares stories of domestic abuse and childhood trauma in the hope of erasing the stigma surrounding these topics and helping those going through similar situations to feel less alone. Through the endless support of her boyfriend, family, and friends, she feels comfortable embracing her past and sharing her story with those who need it. Laura considers it an honor to have her story featured in the Women Write Now: Women in Trauma *anthology alongside other talented female writers who felt strongly enough to share their voices and their stories.*

THE BODY REMEMBERS

Alexandra Vigue

I was tired of being that mom—frazzled, chaotic, and a bit of a mess. Every day at pickup, I'd look at my friend Nessa, with her perfect hair and designer clothes, and think, *Gawd, what happened to me? I used to be hot. For shit sake, I used to be the person my friends made fun of for trekking across campus in heels! What happened to that girl?*

In a wine-fueled moment of brilliance, I went on a Facebook deep dive and found a picture of my pre-kid self. *Man, 20-year-old Alex was hot,* I thought. *Almost 40-year-old Alex could be too. It might just take a little effort.* Then that other voice popped in my head. The one that's always so quick to shame me and remind me that I should be grateful to be alive, that after everything I've been through, it's selfish to worry about something as vain as appearances.

Well, screw you, I thought. *I want to feel good about my appearance again!*

A few months later, a haircut, Collagen Elixir, and a shit-ton of money spent on hair products symbolized a coming into my own of sorts and an adios to that messy bun, yoga-pant-wearing mom I'd become. The final step was to get perfectly shaped Jillian Harris eyebrows. I booked a microblading appointment, ready to take the $700 plunge.

It didn't matter that COVID was at an all-time high in British Columbia, with over 1,200 cases a day. Never mind the fact that it had been well over a year since I'd had any type of appointment indoors. This wasn't like last year at the dentist when I was handed a form and asked to sign in six places to indicate that I understood my increased risk of exposure to COVID. Instead of signing, I burst into tears and left. No, I wasn't anxious about the pandemic anymore.

On the morning of my eyebrow appointment, I drove 45 minutes out of town. As I walked behind the esthetician down the dimly lit hall, I thought, This is it. *I'm one step closer to Alex 2.0 — Business Babe and Mom.*

"Take a seat," the esthetician said, pointing to a chair as she casually hopped up on the bed across from me. It seemed a bit odd to me that, during a global pandemic, she would sit on the bed that I was eventually supposed to lie down on, but I decided to let it go.

"I'll start by drawing your brows, then we can tweak them before I tattoo them on. Ok?

"Ok."

"It might take a few tries, which is why we have so much time booked." "Sure."

"Hop on up and lie down here."

I tried not to look at her like she'd committed COVID blasphemy as she slid down from the bed and patted the spot where my head would be. I lay down, took a breath, and closed my eyes. In what felt like slow motion, she very carefully lowered the overhead light so that it hovered just above my face. Behind my closed eyelids, I could sense the blinding brightness of the light. Suddenly, I found it increasingly hard to breathe through my three-layer mask. I started to squirm.

"Are you ok?"

"Just a little nervous. I'm fine."

I started to cry. Not huge, convulsing, shaky emotional tears, but big, silent tears—elephant tears, as my family used to call them.

"You're crying."

Shit, I thought.

"I know. I'm ok."

"Are you worried about the procedure?" "No."

Crap.

"Are you sure?"

"Yep, I'm ok," I tried to focus on my breathing to calm myself down.

"I think it's just that I haven't been this close to anyone who I don't know in a long time. I'm fine. I guess I'm more worried about COVID than I thought. It's okay."

But I couldn't stop crying. *What am I going to do? Should I say something? I'm pretty sure she thinks I've lost it.*

"I don't think this is a good day for you to do this."

Shit. Well I guess I'm never going to be able to come back here again. So much for my perfect eyebrows.

"You're probably right."

Crap. I just wiped my eyes five times in the middle of a frickin' pandemic. How many surfaces have I touched since I walked in here?

"Let's do this when you're feeling less nervous."

"Ok, sounds good."

There's no freaking way I'm ever going to be able to come back here. She'll probably call in sick when she hears I've booked an appointment.

"You can come back some other time after you get your vaccine. Ok?"

"I will," I said, gathering my things and bolting out the front door.

Crossing the street, I ripped off my mask, sat down in my car, and let the tears fall some more. I have no idea how long I sat there crying; it could have been five minutes or twenty. When I felt a bit more composed, I drove home, stopping at a Tim Horton's to get a cup of my favourite coffee along the way. *I wonder*, I thought, *if part of the reason I lost it was because I was so close to the hospital?* I never go all the way out there. Without realizing it, I had been avoiding that place like the plague.

I pulled into the driveway and wiped my eyes, cursing myself for forgetting hand sanitizer again.

"That was fast," my husband said.

"I didn't do it. I just started crying and left."

He nodded, a silent understanding passing between us. I was grateful that he knew not to ask anything more about it at that moment.

―――

"I think I had a trauma response the other day," I blurted out to my counsellor on our next Zoom Call.

"You *think*?"

Leave it to Lizette to call me out on my shit. "Fine. I had a trauma response the other day."

"Do you want to tell me about it?"

"I had this brilliant idea—don't judge me for being vain—to get my eyebrows microbladed. But when I got there, I couldn't do it. I just started crying. It was like the goddamn dentist all over again."

"When did you start crying?"

"When I was lying there, and I couldn't breathe through my mask, and she lowered this light in front of my face."

"It makes a lot of sense to me that you got upset."

"I guess."

"You guess?" She gave me that Lizette look again, the one that said she knew I was full of shit.

"Fine. Yes, it makes sense." I loved and hated that she could read me so well.

"What were you thinking about when she lowered the light?"

"I don't know."

There was that look again. I guess I was going to have to tell her.

"Ok. The whole ride home I just kept thinking about this time that's so fuzzy. I'm not even sure if I'm remembering one thing or a blend of things. Like, I remember blinding lights and wondering if I was dying, then hearing my aunt's voice. I know now that that's the day I got my tracheotomy. Anyway, I couldn't move, and I felt like there were people there, but no one was paying attention to me."

"Where were the people?"

"In front of me. My aunt was on the side."

"On what side?"

"The right. On my drive home I kept thinking about the blinding lights, my aunt talking, and how I wanted to move but I couldn't."

"You were in a medically induced coma, right?" "Yes."

"There's a certain amount of awareness that's considered acceptable when someone's in an induced coma. Maybe you were in and out of consciousness."

"Do you think I was supposed to be awake? Like was I supposed to remember a trach surgery?"

"No, I definitely don't think you were supposed to remember it. Is that what you think you're remembering?"

"Do you think that's what I'm remembering?"

"I don't know," she said, clearly not willing to do the work for me. "Ok, let's try this. Think back to that time. What did your body want to do?"

"Blink," I replied.

"Interesting," she said. "Put yourself back in the hospital on that day."

I hated visualizing but went along. I picture myself lying on a bed, with tears running down my face. Nobody seems to notice. I can hear people talking, but I'm not sure where the voices are coming from. My first thought is, *I have a cold. Pneumonia. Maybe it's swine flu. Wouldn't that be ironic if the biggest self-proclaimed hypochondriac in the world has H1N1! I must have died from it. Or maybe I AM dying from it. It's really bright here.*

I can't see anything because the light is blinding, and I want to blink or open my eyes, but I can't. I hear my aunt Chris. *Chris is here,* I think, *I must be fine.*

"Are you there?" Lizette asked, bringing me back to the present. "Yes."

"I want you to blink. Don't stop blinking until your body naturally stops, ok? It might feel uncomfortable."

"Ok," I said, then I start blinking.

"Now, turn your head to the right and left. Keep turning it to either side, and don't stop blinking."

I blink and blink. I turn my head to the right, and I blink faster and faster.

"Keep blinking and turning your head."

Suddenly something releases. I can't explain it, but a deep pressure behind my right eye just snaps like a rubber band, and the blinking slows to nothing. I open my mouth to speak, but Lizette beats me to it.

"Take a minute, Alex. Sit with whatever feelings you're having in your body right now before you say anything."

"Ok."

"How do you feel?" "Relieved. Calm."

"Great. Are you open to hearing what I noticed?"

"Sure."

"Every time you turned your head to the right, you blinked faster and faster. That's the side you said your aunt was on, right?"

"Yes. I noticed that too. Do you think that's why I had a traumatic response?" "Are you asking for my best guess?"

"Yes."

"If I had to guess, I'd say that at that moment when the esthetician shone the light on your face and you felt like you couldn't breathe, your mind and body remembered the feeling of having been in this position before, when it didn't go well, when it wasn't ok. Your mind and body are designed to protect you."

"So, I froze?"

"Well, maybe for a second. But you got up and left, right?"

"Yes. So, how do I let go of all that held body trauma?"

"You allow your body to do the thing it wasn't allowed to do when you were in the hospital. You get up and walk away."

That night I couldn't sleep. I kept thinking about how it's been 11 years since I was hospitalized with H1N1 and that I've spent many of those years believing that the worst part of my two-year recovery started when I woke up in the ICU. After all, it's the part of the six-month hospital journey that I consciously remember. Waking up and feeling scared and sad after discovering I'd been in a comma for six weeks and had lost a lung. Enduring endless breathing trials while hooked up to a ventilator for four long months. Being unable to lift even my hand because my muscles had atrophied while I was in the coma. Learning to sit and walk all over again.

Those six weeks in a coma, though—when my body fought to survive—I had somehow convinced myself that those weren't all that impactful to me. I was so sure that my time in the coma didn't affect me, mostly because I didn't remember it. It was my family's journey and experience, not mine. I let myself believe that those six weeks were insignificant to me. It took a new global pandemic for me to realize that that girl on life support, dying from H1N1, wasn't some *Grey's Anatomy* character that I could pity and watch from a distance. She was me. And everything my body went through during that time—all the physical trauma it endured—didn't happen to some fictional character. It happened to me.

The day after my counselling session, I stood and looked at myself in the mirror. *Holy shit*, I thought, *my right eye looks bigger*. I leaned closer just to be sure. It looked less droopy, and brighter too! Maybe my body really had released whatever it had been holding on to. Maybe the blinking was really what it needed. I thought back to that breath work course I'd recently taken. *Hadn't I had a similar experience then?* As I lay breathing through that class, I found myself thinking again of the ICU. I thought about how I had spent so many days throughout my recovery feeling like my body had failed me and questioning over and over again why it had failed. Lying there, my body started to shake, and I cried.

"Your body is amazing" someone once told me after my near-death experience. I brushed off the remark like it was no big deal. Crying in my breath work class, her words came flooding back to me. At that moment, it hit me how strong my body truly is. This vessel had been as close to the brink of death as humanly possible, as rooms full of physicians had told me over and over again. It had fought on life support for six weeks, hooked up to a machine that pumped my blood into a tube to oxygenate before circling back into my body. It came back from the dead when I flatlined and a doctor pumped on my heart for a minute and a half, refusing to let me die. It survived a surgery where I had a 20 percent chance of survival. In that moment, it hit me that this body is a lot stronger than I have ever given it credit for. In fact, my body is pretty amazing.

The other day I listened to a news story about a 20-year-old guy who talked about "thumping" during his stay in the ICU with COVID. Thumping is this terrible process whereby a respiratory therapist literally thumps on your back until you cough up phlegm. It's a twisted version of burping a baby. It's disgusting but necessary to rid the infection that sits deep in the lungs which, if left alone, would cause pneumonia. I listened to him talk, and I was transported back to room number 5 at Royal Columbian Hospital—to respiratory therapists thumping on my back; to the horrible feeling of suction; to not being able to breathe; to hours of breathing trials where it felt like I was fighting for each breath, only gaining relief when I was hooked back up to a ventilator. That's what recovering from respiratory failure looks like. If you recover.

The day I left the hospital after six long months, one of my favourite nurses said, "Alex, you've been given a gift. Don't waste it. You've been given this amazing second chance at life." I loved her, and she meant well, but looking back, I realize those words have put a lot of pressure on me over the last 11 years. Never feeling like what I'm doing or who I am is enough. Every day I think about people with COVID being released from the ICU. I picture their families' joy over their recovery. I picture them being told how lucky they are—a medical miracle when so many others around them have died. I wonder what we're doing to help them process the journey both their minds and bodies have gone through. Like me, are any of them wondering if they'll ever do anything worthy enough, or deserving enough, to have simply been one of the lucky ones to have survived?

———————

Alexandra is a copywriter and editor who lives in Vancouver, British Columbia, Canada. She is a reader and avid writer who is excited to be part of this project with amazing women from around the world.

PAIN, DEATH, AND A HORSE

Gretchen Mayer-Yeh

It was the beginning of December. The air was cold, the trees' bare brown branches stretched up to the gray sky in grotesque shapes, begging the sun to shine. I was in the house and had just finished my lunch. I had two more hours of piano practicing left; I was preparing for music school auditions. At the time, there were so many things on my mind; the girls at the pretzel store I worked at and their drama, the music I was practicing, and my own personal struggles.

My dad called me into the office. As a young child, I used to find the office a dreaded place that I never wanted to enter because painful punishment was always applied inside the small square room. When I grew out of the spanking stage, the office became the place of intense discussions with my parents. When my dad called me into the office, I knew that we were going to have an intense discussion, and I knew that it was going to be about my horse.

As long as I can remember, I loved horses. My sister and I shared the same passion for horses and often played together in a land we made up called (ironically enough) "Horseland." My sister and I bought horse magazines, collected Grand Champion and Breyer horse figurines, put posters of horses on the walls of our bedroom, and begged my dad for a horse. When I was nine, we got our first pony. Eventually, we sold the pony and bought the pregnant black mare that became my horse.

Recently, my horse Night had been suffering from lameness; I couldn't ride her at all. Because of her lameness, we had her hooves

X-rayed at the vet's clinic and discovered that she had a disease known as navicular syndrome, which is basically disintegration of the bones in the hoof. This diagnosis meant that my horse was permanently lame at the young age of fourteen. Her lameness and pain would only get worse.

The first few months after the diagnosis, my sister and I spent time researching navicular syndrome and trying to find re-homing options for my horse. My sister was already in college, and I was going to college the following year. My parents and brothers were not able to care for our horses, and we were going to have to find re-homing options either way.

Night's hoof disease only complicated the situation. Unfortunately, Night had a hot temper, and we knew she wouldn't do well in most situations. We had trouble finding re-homing options because, at that time, the market was flooded with horses, and no one had space or money to house a lame horse. There were special shoes we could buy from the farrier for Night's hooves, but they were expensive and would be a short-term solution at best. I knew we were running out of options for her.

I sat across from my dad on his favorite blue easy chair. He sat at his large computer desk. I fidgeted in my seat and tried not to look him in the eye. I felt like I had a weight sitting in my stomach; I knew what was coming.

My dad started the conversation. "Gretchen, I want to talk to you about your horse. I think we should put her down."

My first reaction: tears. I'm sure my dad was expecting it; he knew I loved Night. But I don't think he quite realized how much I loved her. I sat for a while in the office, crying and telling my dad about my horse, how I had worked with her, how I had spent time with her, how I had trained her, how I was the only one who believed that she could become an amazing horse to ride, how I knew that it was the right thing to put her down, and how I didn't want to put her down.

I talked more and more about my horse (in between sobs), but instead of calming down I became more worked up. Finally, I got up from my seat and ran out of the office and out to the barn. There was my horse, her white stripe running down her nose with the snip that always appeared in the winter and disappeared in the summer. She simply looked at me, her fuzzy ears cocked toward me. Night didn't know what was going on; she didn't know why I was crying. She didn't know that I had just decided to take away her life.

I sat down by her stall door and cried uncontrollably until my dad came looking for me. He helped me calm down and took me back inside the house where I tried to hide my red eyes from my four brothers' inquisitive gazes.

That episode was only the beginning of the nightmarish week that followed. Although the situation was always nagging in the back of my mind, I tried not to think about Night. I was busy and tried to keep my mind off of the horrible decision I had made; I had school, work and piano practice. There was no time to think about my beloved animal being put down. But whenever I went out to the barn, I was always smacked in the face with the realization that soon I would never, ever see my horse again. I would never ride her again, never feel her nervous excitement underneath her saddle. I would never again rock back and forth with her as she cantered. I would never be able to bend down in the saddle and feel her muscles ripple underneath my fingers as she changed gaits. I would never again feel the oneness that I always felt with her when I rode her.

I also had to deal with the realization that my childhood dreams of horses were over. I knew I wasn't going to get another horse after this one. She was it. We had another horse, her son Scout. But that horse was my sister's. He wasn't mine. I didn't train him. I hardly ever rode him. I always took care of, rode, and trained my own horse, Night.

The day before my horse was put down, I tromped through the slushy snow out to the barn with my camera and took pictures of her. I wanted to have memories of every special white marking, every scar, every bit of her. I even took a picture of her tail because she always had such a beautiful, full black tail. When I was out there with her, I cried, cried harder than I had ever cried in my life. I felt like I was saying goodbye to one of my dearest friends. I felt like a dagger had carved out a little part of my heart and thrown it away where it could never be retrieved. I felt alone. I felt like I had no choice but to give up the animal that I had spent so much time with and worked so hard to train and had loved so much.

The day my horse was put down, I had to work at the pretzel store in the mall. Before I left, I ran out to the barn with my family's German Shepherd tagging at my heels like it was a normal day. But I knew that it would never be normal again. I would never run out to the barn again to see my horse. When it would be time for me to feed the cats and Scout that night, I knew there would be one horse missing and a bit of me would be missing too.

I went to my horse's stall and stood there, staring at her. I had to leave; I knew that I would be late for work. I looked into her large, innocent brown eyes. She didn't know what was going to happen. I remember praying that Night would put her nose up to my lips so I could blow into her nostrils; she often did this to me to "tell" me that I was her boss. I loved her so much. She put her nose up to my mouth for the last time and I blew into her nostrils, tears streaming down my face. I left my horse, knowing that I would never see her again. I remember the ache inside of me was so enormous that I screamed in pain as I walked out of the barn. If you knew me, you would know that screaming doesn't come naturally for me. Growing up, I never screamed when someone scared me, and I never screamed on roller coasters. The screams just wouldn't come. Sometimes I would yelp, but never anything loud enough to brag about. The day I left my horse for the last time, I screamed.

After I had worked for a few hours at the pretzel store, I made the mistake of calling my mom to see if the vet had come to kill my horse. He had. I hung up quickly and told my co-worker, "I have to go to the bathroom." I went into the small bathroom, closed the door, and crouched close to the ground in the utter darkness, covering my head with my hands and sobbing.

The date December 15, 2021, was fifteen years since my horse was put down. It took me several years not to cry every time I came across the photos I took of her the day before she was put down. I still have her halter. I get it out from time to time and remember her smooth-as-glass canter and the bond we had. For a while, I tried to forget my love for horses, but gradually the ache to be near them came back. I now go riding occasionally and maybe I will eventually get to own a horse again, but there will never be another horse like Night.

Gretchen Mayer-Yeh is a pianist, copywriter, and adjunct professor who holds a master's degree in piano performance. She has had several articles and interviews published in music magazines such as Sax Magazine, Bass Magazine, *and* Piano Magazine. *She also contributed to* Western Humanities and Christian Thought *published by Kendall Hunt. In her spare time, Gretchen enjoys reading, writing, and baking.*

TURNING PAIN INTO POWER

Julie Bilotta

Growing up I could have never imagined that one day my life would be plastered on the front of the newspaper or featured on the 6 o'clock news. Reading and hearing about yourself really is a strange feeling. It also is extremely frustrating when the story being told is sprinkled with half-truths and salacious titles. But that's what the media does best and whether we'd like to admit it or not, we're more likely to tune in to or read about a scandal. Everyone loves a good scandal. Hell, I'd be lying if I said I didn't love a good scandal. But the tables really turn when you become that scandal. And all these internet nobodies want to chime in on what they think of you and tell you how awful you are. Think of the most awful thing you can in your head, and I promise I've probably heard it said about me. That's one thing that I was always used to—living in small city where everybody knows everybody or at least knows your name. For some weird reason people have always spoken about me—good or bad, I've heard it all—but never on the magnitude of international headlines. But to understand how we got here, I have to take you back. Behind every story, there are always many events that led up to it. I mean we don't all end up in jail at 8 months pregnant and go on to being forced into giving birth breech in solitary confinement in a room full of correctional officers. But I did. So let's go back in time.

If you asked me to describe myself in one word, I'd go with bold. If you asked someone else, they might say something dramatic or a cunt. Guess it depends who you ask lol (can you say lol in a book?). Either way I don't care and to be honest I never have. I've always been extremely outspoken for as long as I can remember. I was born in Toronto and lived there until my parents split when I was two. My mother and I moved back to her hometown which is Cornwall, a city with about 60,000 people, located next to the Akwesasne reservation—small enough to where you could drive from one end of town to the other in 5 minutes—small enough where everyone knows everyone or knows someone who knows that person. You get the drift—a city that really doesn't have much to offer to kids and teens to keep them busy—one mall, a few grocery stores and St Lawrence College.

For the most part I would say I was a good kid. I went to a French school even though neither of my parents can speak French. My mother is Canadian, was born in Italy and moved here when she was 7. My mother wanted me to be able to speak both English and French as we lived on the border of Quebec, so it would be useful in the future when it came to getting jobs in a mainly French dominated province. Fun fact—French is the second language in Canada. Surprisingly, I did well learning it and can still speak it to this day.

I know we definitely change as we get older, but a lot for me has stayed the same. For example, pink is still my favourite colour, playing with makeup is still so fun to me, and I still talk way too much and don't know when to shut up. No seriously—ask anyone who knows me. If you think you're getting off the phone in less than an hour when you called just to ask a simple question, then you'd be mistaken. Honestly, I was a pretty good kid who listened to her parents and didn't really get into much trouble. As I got closer to my teenage years, the attitude really started and the sneaking out and staying up all night on a school night talking on a landline 'til either I got caught or I hung up and pretended to sleep so I wouldn't get caught. If you know you know. I always wanted to act or be older than I was. I think that's the case for a lot of us until you have to choose between your Sephora order or paying the electricity bill. Not going to lie—I've definitely strayed more towards what I wanted versus what I needed.

Nothing really crazy happened until the infamous breaking of the ankle and the lawsuit that my mothered filed after it, as I was only 13. I call it infamous because today at 35 people still talk about it. So, 13 is when the boy crazy stage started and the sneaking out to meet friends at the Riverdale park. It was also the first time trying weed and smoking a cigarette. I was 14 or 15 when things really popped off. High school is when I started being the ultimate nightmare for any parents—ask mine—they'll tell you. I started high school at a catholic school St Joe's. Hated it and begged my mom to let me go to St Lawrence as that's where most of my friends at the time were. Got my way and stayed for a semester. Hated it and went back to St Joe's. Still hated it. There was also another high school that was connected to ours with a shared cafeteria. I ended up making friends there, and, you guessed it, I transferred there. For the most part I liked it. However, this is when I really started drinking and having parties at my house when my mom wasn't home. I drove around with older friends because, as a teen, unless you were in sports, there really wasn't anything else to do. This is also when lots of girls started hating me. A lot of them I didn't know. People calling me on my little blue cell phone to tell me off was a regular thing—so was my mother's house getting egged and vandalized. Some idiot even spray painted it. You know who you are and I still think you're an idiot.

My mom worked a lot, so this gave me all the time I needed to get myself involved with all the wrong friends, boys and people. I was exposed to a lot at a young age—drug deals, and I'm not talking just a gram of weed, but I'm also not talking to get myself arrested, so make of that what you will. But I didn't bat an eye. It was normal around here. Looking back on it now, I can see exactly where I started going off the rails and why this was so normalized to me. I remember being in a hotel bathroom one night and this girl I had been friends with took a little bag. Inside was coke. I vividly remember her pouring out a few little bugs onto the lid of the toilet, pulling out a rolled-up bill and doing it. She looked up and offered it to me. I was terrified of drugs and being only barely 15, this was a big deal. She was a year younger than I was and I was honestly scared, but that was the first time I tried it. I remember praying that nothing bad would happen to either of us. I'm so sorry, Mom—I'll probably say this a lot. I remember vowing to never touch it again and for a long time that would remain true.

I eventually got expelled from school for "being too much of a bad influence on other students"—not my words, but the principal's. It sucked because I liked it there—not because of the actual stuff you're supposed to be in school for, but because of my friends who were my whole life at that age. I tried a few times to go places that offered classes so I could get my grade 12, but that never happened. I was too busy partying and doing everything I shouldn't have been. By 16 I had caught my first charge—assault causing bodily harm. The other girl didn't show up to court and the charges were dropped. That was my first run-in with the law. I was also living and bouncing from friend to friend's house because my mom wasn't happy with my behaviour and I don't blame her. Mom, I'm sorry—I know you know, but I really put you through it. I had my own apartment for a month that one of my friends gave me the money for, and it was basically just a party place. I had a roommate, but by the end of the month we were both begging to go back home and we did. I still wasn't listening and things were getting progressively worse. I did what I wanted when I wanted and I was completely out of control. There were really no repercussions at home because, as a single mom with a second child who was only 5 at the time, I think Mom didn't know what to do with me. This is also when I started learning how to make money the fast way. No, I'm not talking about stripping either. I know that was a rumour since being with the "right" people got me into those places, too—a big shout out to all the strippers as they were really nice girls! I'm sure they were single moms or putting themselves through school.

I was seeking validation in all the wrong places and any attention was good attention to me. At 18 I had received the money from when I had broken my ankle as a child and I bought myself a mustang and turned the whole thing into a pink barbie dream. So, looking back on it, I get why girls specifically were jealous and always talked about me. I always had the nicest clothes and the nicest cars that I really didn't have to work for. I was living a life by that point where seeing someone count out $100,000 on their coffee table while someone else was doing line after line of cocaine off the kitchen table was just normal. I just wanted to have money like that and be "successful" like that. Little did I know I was a just a kid who was about to come face to face with something I still have nightmares about.

At 18 years old I ended up at a home with some guy I didn't know and 20 pounds of weed in a truck that wasn't mine, and I just had this horrible feeling. Even the night before I had this gut feeling that something wasn't right and something bad was about to happen. Side note: Always listen to your intuition—you have it for a reason and had I listened to mine, what happened next probably wouldn't be part of this story. I remember driving with this stranger and these little jeeps were following us. One would get off and another one would get behind us. Did I mention I was in Syracuse, New York? Zero tolerance for anything to do with drugs. I didn't know that then but I sure do now. We went to this random house that he directed me to, and I remember walking into this gross house with little children walking around, and he sits down and starts doing lines of coke. I look outside and I can see the under-cover cops moving in on the house. I remember telling him that we were about to get busted and his saying, "Well it's not my weed—it's yours." I was so upset and scared but before I could even utter another syllable, the whole house was filled with cops. I was thrown to the ground, knee in my back and a gun to my head while being handcuffed. I was thrown into the back of a cop car and driven to a police station where I sat handcuffed waiting for whatever was to come next. I briefly remember 2 drug task force agents coming in and asking me a bunch of questions about what belonged to whom and everything you can picture an interrogation looking like. After being a smart ass and just not giving them what they wanted, I was brought to the Onondoga county jail. It was dingy and gross, and I still hadn't called home to tell either of my parents what was going on. I remember being in this disgusting holding cell with 8 other girls for the first two days. I was so cold and I told the correctional officer that. I can still remember his asking me if I was cold and I said yes as I was still in the same clothes I had been arrested in—a little top from Marciano and a pair of Parasuco jeans. Anyways, he starts laughing and I quote this asshole saying, "Well you picked the wrong motherfucker to give a fuck" and then he walked away. So, two days after being there they let us out of this cement room and into a day room that had phones you could only call landlines on and only to someone who would accept a collect call. I waited a while and then I dialled my mother's number. That was the scariest part because I was still a child who thought my mother was going to be upset but she was really scared as I wasn't even in the country I was from and the laws in the US are way different than they are here in Canada. I ended up going in front of a judge for my bail, and hearing the bail set at $15,000USD was terrifying. Two days later I would be on my way back home, and I couldn't have been more excited to see my mother's face. It was far from over as I was only on bail, but for the time being that was fine. I ended up with an amazing attorney from New York City, and he was able to get the case thrown out on a discrepancy in the paperwork. However, I was told that I couldn't come back to US for 10 years and had to pay a $5,000 fine. I'll be honest…I almost didn't even go to the final court date. My lawyer told me I wasn't going to do time and that everything was going to be ok. I was so fucking scared at the thought of it going wrong and having to do time in that gross jail—it was something I didn't think I could handle. But I went and I did go home that day. I remember promising my parents and myself that I would never do anything like this again. And if that had been the truth, then you wouldn't be reading this now, would you?

I came home and nothing really changed except for the fact that I could no longer go to the States which really did suck at the time because so many people I was friends with lived on that side of the reservation, in addition to missing my lavish trips to NYC and Miami. Through all this, I still wasn't using drugs and I never actually liked weed—it just gave me anxiety. Regardless, I was still this arrogant, ignorant little bitch that knew it all and you couldn't tell me different. I was still driving this flashy pink car that everyone knew was mine, including the local police who were pulling me over on a daily basis, even multiple times a day. Every time I would act out and make a scene. It's embarrassing now looking back on it. I was a nightmare to deal with. I thought I knew everything and you couldn't tell me otherwise. I knew I didn't have anything illegal in the car and instead of making things easy, I would demand warrants to pop the trunk and threaten lawsuits. I thought I was being targeted and my dumb ass really thought I didn't deserve it. *No, Julie, it has nothing to do with the high-profile drug dealers that you're known to be friends with. It has nothing to do with being involved with all the wrong people. Poor Julie—you're just getting pulled over for nothing.* I'm seriously cringing so hard thinking of the way I behaved then. I probably would have hated me too. I was so angry and confrontational. I was in a terrible relationship that was highly physically abusive—something that I had never experienced before. Getting punched in the face or kicked in the ribs because I wanted to go to my grandfather's funeral 4 hours away was normal. I must have done something wrong. After a horrible year and a half, the relationship would end and I emerged a different person. In a lot of ways, I was relieved that I wasn't constantly apologizing for things I didn't owe an apology for. However, I decided to deal with that train wreck of a year by drinking almost every other night and going out with my friends.

Sooner than later, I was in my next extremely toxic relationship, which included tons of gaslighting and being cheated on, ghosted for a week at a time while he was going back and forth with his ex. This is when I started taking percocets every day. They made all my problems go away, or so I thought. At least for the time being I could escape my reality and forget about my problems. Getting high on pain killers was a whole new thing to me. I had never felt anything like it and horrifyingly enough I enjoyed the way I felt. I wasn't crying anymore or starving myself because I felt so sick and anxiety ridden from being in such a toxic relationship where I constantly blamed myself. *I must not be a good enough girlfriend. I'm not skinny enough* (except I was almost down to 100 pounds). *I'm not pretty enough.* I just wasn't enough. Except I was and I wasn't the problem. I just couldn't see my own worth because I had placed my self-worth in someone else. Side note: Please don't ever think your worth lies with the thoughts of a man or woman, or anyone for that fact. Anyways, as the relationship got worse so did my drug abuse. The percocets weren't doing what they used to. Unbeknownst to me, I was building a tolerance and I was now addicted. However, if you had asked me then I would have told you I could stop anytime… only that couldn't have been any further from the truth. I think I got up to 26 percocets a day and was told that oxycontin was way better and I would only have to take one or two and so that's what I did. BIGGEST mistake of my life. At that time, they were being marketed as non-addictive which was the biggest bold-faced lie ever told. They were not only addictive—they were literally life ruining pills.

As you can imagine I was starting to abuse these now. I was taking upwards of 10 oxycontins a day. I was out of control. But hey, I wasn't sad, so it was fine—only it really wasn't. As you probably know, addicts will do pretty much anything for money to support these expensive habits and when I was offered a large amount of money to drive 50 pounds of weed less than an hour away for a few thousand, I did it. This would turn out to be another one of the biggest mistakes I had ever made in my life. On my way home I just had this feeling that something wasn't right. Someone I knew kept calling me, asking me where I was but since I thought this person was my closest friend, I didn't think anything of it— only this person was reporting back to the police and within half an hour I would be surrounded by police.

I still remember that gut feeling, that feeling deep down inside that you just can't ignore. It was obviously my intuition telling me that things were about to go left real quick. I had that feeling on my way to this place, and I chose not to listen. Please always listen to your intuition. I wish I had that day. Anyways, within minutes I was surrounded at an abandoned toll booth, with a bunch of undercover police officers screaming at me to get out of the car.

I remember telling them they needed a warrant and that they had no right to search my vehicle. Regardless the gig was up, and an officer walked over and popped the trunk to unveil garbage bags full to the brim with weed. I was swiftly placed under arrest and my co-conspirator was taken away. Just like that my life would be a living nightmare. Nothing would be the same and things weren't going to get any better any time soon.

That night is still kind off blur. Whether it was the ridiculous amount of pain meds I was abusing or just the sheer fact of shock, I don't remember much. I know they wanted so desperately to find oxy's or any kind of pain med. Apparently the police had a whole task force dedicated to taking me down. I don't blame them. I also don't blame myself. I was a broken, depressed addict and it was everyone else's fault but my own.

———

Enter my first stay at the Ottawa Carleton Detention Centre (OCDC). I still remember my first night there. I was so scared to be in a cell by myself. I didn't want to be alone—period. Any form of human contact was welcome. I really thought I'd be there a night, maybe two, and then I'd be home. I clearly wasn't taking this seriously. To me 50 pounds of weed was just that—a drop in the bucket, a drug that didn't hurt anyone.

I remember being so annoyed and mad at the police for putting me in this situation. The entitlement is real, isn't it? Like I wasn't responsible and my actions weren't the reason for this. *Nope...blame it on anyone and everyone else but yourself, Julie.*

The next two weeks weren't horrible. I already knew people in there and I wasn't withdrawing because you can get any drug you want on the inside. Make no mistake, anything you can think of from sleeping pills to cocaine was available. It might cost you a few chocolate bars. Yes, food is used to buy these things...or money deposited in someone's account. The worst part was getting up at 4 am for court and sitting in a giant metal box that would transport you to your lovely holding cell in Cornwall or wherever your court appearance was. I remember sitting there just waiting for my name to be called and time just going by so slowly. Sitting in the holding cells at the court house made the jail look like a 5-star resort. My name was finally called and it was time for my bail hearing. A bunch of legal jargon later, I was out on a $15,000 bail with my mother as my surety which is basically someone who signs under penalty of the bail amount to see that you follow all your bail conditions and show up to court. Can we talk about my bail release conditions for a second? Who am I asking lol—this is my story so of course we can! I wasn't to be anywhere without my mother. This meant that I could no longer live in this overpriced house I was renting. Now I would be sleeping on my mom's couch. I would not be allowed to leave for even a second without my mother being present. I couldn't be around anyone who was known to use drugs or consume any drugs that were not prescribed to me—such a stupid condition and surefire way to put any addict such as myself right back where she started—but more on that later.

I was home and out of that dirty, disgusting jail and was just happy to take a shower and put on some clean clothes. I also needed to find someone who had drugs so I wouldn't withdraw as it was getting to that point where I was starting to feel awful. Yup, already breaching my conditions and putting my own mother on the line for $15,000.

After my release, I sat down with both my parents and told them the ugly truth about my addiction. They really didn't know much about opioids at the time, but they soon found out. They didn't know how much control my addiction had over my life, but believe me, they learned that I had absolutely no control anymore because the drugs did. And to be honest, I don't think I knew either, because up until then I was making fast money and was able to support my addiction.

We went back and forth trying to figure something out when the topic of methadone came up. I agreed to start the program to make them happy, but the truth was I had no intention of stopping. One thing you have to know about addiction is that if someone doesn't want help, you can't make them get help.

As soon as my parents went to sleep, I called someone I knew. Within the hour I had a few oxycontins in my hand, which at that time was my drug of choice.

However, I was on such strict conditions that I was basically broke and having a really hard time supporting this habit.

That's when I started to acknowledge this little blue pill was running my life.

That's when the lying and stealing started.

Even if I wanted to stop, I couldn't. I was too scared to go through the withdrawals and I wasn't ready to deal with reality.

Fast forward to the summer. I had snuck out of the house and gone to a house party while my mom was asleep. I was still hanging around with all the wrong people. Someone whom I considered to be a friend and who was also a drug user had stolen jewelry. She had no ID and promised me half the money if I went to the pawn shop to get rid of it. I knew it was wrong, but at the time I was in so far over my head I really didn't care.

A few weeks later, I was contacted by the person who threw the party and was told that this "friend" had put it all on me, and if the jewelry was not returned, they would go ahead with charges. The jewelry was long gone at this point, and even if I did want to give it back, I didn't have the money to get it out. So, they followed through with charges and issued a warrant for my arrest.

By this time, I was the worst I'd ever been. I knew my mom had signed a bond for $15,000 and if she didn't report me for what I was doing, and if I was caught breaching the conditions of my release, she would lose the money. She knew how bad I was at this point, but she didn't want to turn me in. However, I wasn't following the conditions at all; I wasn't even living with her anymore. I didn't care about anything or anyone, as awful as that sounds. A few times police went to her door looking for me and she made excuses and covered for me. My heart breaks every time I think of what I put her through.

At the end of the summer, some of my friends who were not users came by to see me. They knew right away I wasn't the same person anymore. I lied. I tried everything to get them to leave. From what I'm told, they came back later that day to check on me and found me lying in my bed and unresponsive.

Not knowing what to do, my friends called my mother. She called an ambulance and, because it was drug-related, the police were also called. I snapped out of it when I heard her on the phone and ran to a neighbour's house and asked them to call a taxi. I knew that I'd be going back to jail.

I made it to a friend's house. About ten minutes later, the whole street was covered with police and I was arrested on the spot. They took me to the hospital and then back to jail I went—only now I had four new charges which were provincial offenses.

The first week was honestly a blur to me. I was experiencing withdrawals for the first time. I was placed on medical observation.

I've never been so sick in my entire life. These withdrawals carried on for almost three weeks. This time around there were no drugs; I had no choice but to deal with it. My parents had decided that they weren't going to bail me out, that it was best for me to sit there and dry out. At the time I was really upset with them, but I know now that they did it because they loved me and they didn't want to see me end up dead.

Eventually I had gotten used to being in jail—well, as used to it as you can get. I was offered a plea deal of four months in jail for what I had done. Thinking about it now, being incarcerated then probably saved my life. I accepted the deal because waiting for a trial meant I could be sitting there for a year waiting for my day in court. This is why so many people end up pleading, even sometimes to things they haven't done. To me, it's another sneaky trick the courts play with people who are incarcerated. It's a quick way to get a conviction against you.

I completed my time but here's the tricky part: I was still waiting to go to trial on my federal charges. I was there for a little over four months and the conditions inside the jail were pretty awful. It was filthy and overcrowded. More often than not we were three people to a cell that was only meant to hold two. I learned really fast not to ask the guards for anything. I've actually heard guards tell other inmates not to knock on the door unless someone's dying. I knew that in order to survive in there you had to do as they said, even if it was wrong.

Going to jail isn't meant to be a fun experience by any means; it's a form of punishment. But that does not give guards the right to treat you like dirt. I caught on very quickly that the guards run the show and to keep your mouth shut. If they didn't so much as like the look on your face, they'd be sending you to the hole, aka solitary confinement.

After being in jail for over four months, I had time served on my provincial charges but my federal charges were still pending. That meant that I would have to go for bail again. Sometime in

October I went for bail and the judge denied it. I would have to wait thirty days to reapply in Superior Court.

My mother could no longer be my surety because I had broken the law on her watch, so this time my uncle volunteered. When it was my turn to explain to the judge why I should be let out, I explained that I had been battling with addiction and that I took the time in jail to get sober. I had learned my lesson and I just wanted to be home with my family. The crown, on the other hand, was fighting to keep me incarcerated.

I still remember waiting for the judge's decision. He decided to give me another chance, but if I thought the first set of conditions were strict, the new conditions brought it to a whole new level.

Not only could I not leave the house without my surety, I had to literally go to work with him. At that time my uncle was an independent contractor. I had to keep a diary of my weekly activities and submit it to the court. I was not to be left alone for any reason, not even at home, and because I had a 10 pm curfew, that meant my uncle did too. The only time I was allowed to go anywhere alone was to any drug-related treatment or counseling. I was honestly surprised my uncle even agreed to it.

We both signed the paperwork, and within a couple of hours I was walking out of the courtroom and moving in with my uncle. A few weeks into this I met Dakota, the man who would one day be Gionni's father. Because I couldn't leave, he would visit a lot. We couldn't really do normal things couples do because I couldn't go anywhere without my chaperone.

About three months later, I got a knock at the door and it was two police officers. I hadn't done anything wrong so I invited them inside. They told me that they had grounds for my arrest. My heart dropped. They told me that someone had made a complaint that I was at the grocery store without my surety. I tried explaining that he was there, but as we were walking in, he had received a phone call, so I had gone inside to get what he needed.

They weren't going to listen to anything I had to say. My mother was there and she and my uncle were pleading with them not to arrest me, telling them how good I was doing, that I was staying sober and was following my conditions.

I have really bad anxiety, so with all the commotion going on I ran upstairs and hid in my uncle's room. The police later said that I had left the residence, when they never even checked to see if I was there in the first place. This added on a total of four new breaches.

About three weeks later, the police came with a warrant and I was taken back to jail. This would be my third time in OCDC. When you first get there, a nurse asks you questions about your health. You're also asked if there is a possibility that you may be pregnant. I didn't think that I was, but I told the nurse that it could be possible. I did a urine sample and really didn't give it another thought.

—

I was depressed—being back there for something I hadn't done. I remember this like it was yesterday. Around 10 pm, a guard came to my cell and brought me out to the day room where a nurse was waiting for me. She told me that my pregnancy test had come back positive.

I was completely shocked. A million different emotions went through my mind. I went back to my cell and thought about it all night. In the morning I called home and told my mother and my boyfriend the news. Everyone was so happy and I was too. Now I was eager to get home and be with my family.

For the first week or two I was going back and forth to court. When I came back one night, the guards told me I was switching cells. I didn't even know where I was going until I was led to a segregation cell. I was told they had a suspicion that I had drugs on me and that I would be "dry celled". This means that you are left alone in a cell with no running water. They take your mattress from nine in the morning until nine at night and literally leave you with a blanket and a bible. Keep in mind, these people knew I was pregnant, but they couldn't have cared less. You have no human contact and you aren't allowed to call anyone except a lawyer.

This kind of punishment is cruel and unusual and it really should only be used as a last resort. At OCDC, it's a regular thing. Being in jail in and of itself, locked in a cell for 23 hours a day, is hard enough, so you can only imagine how hard it is to be locked in a small room with no windows, no other inmates, and literally nothing to do but think.

I called my lawyer and asked him if he could contact the jail and see if there was any way out of this. Was that ever a mistake. I literally had guards laugh in my face, and I bet they kept me segregated for even longer because I had told someone what they were doing to me. There's no point in complaining to anyone while you're in there because until the day you get to leave, they have complete control over what they do to you.

Twenty-one days later I was placed back into general population. I stayed in cell block, which was considered "maximum security", for a couple of weeks, and then was placed in a dorm which was considered a privilege. Basically, it's a big room with sixteen bunk beds, three phones that you can use from morning until 9 pm and a TV which is allowed to be kept on until 11 pm, or 2 am during the weekends.

I was offered a plea deal of thirty days, which I had already done by this time, but if I pled guilty, my uncle would have had to pay a $5,000 bond because this would be an admission of guilt on my part. I spoke with my lawyer, Don Johnson, and asked him to get me a fast trial date. It would be a total of three months before I would finally go to court.

My day in court finally came and I ended up beating all charges, which meant I would be re-released on my uncle's watch. Unfortunately, my uncle decided he no longer wanted that responsibility. To my utter dismay, he revoked his surety the following morning, and I was taken back into custody until someone else could be found.

I was absolutely devastated at this point and also about four months pregnant. All week, my mother and Dakota were trying to find someone who would be willing to be my surety and to live by the conditions of the court.

Dakota's aunt decided she would sign to be my surety. After the lawyer spoke with the crown attorney, he decided that she would be suitable and a little over a week later we were back in court in front of another judge. She changed some of my conditions, but they basically remained the same: I wasn't to leave the residence without her and I was to reside with her until my matters before the court were resolved.

My first day at her home, we realized quickly there was literally nowhere for me to stay because her apartment was so small. She told me that I'd have to find somewhere else to stay because there was no room for me at her home.

Again, my living anywhere but with her would be in violation of my bail conditions and would send me back to jail—but if that happened, I would most likely be delivering my son in jail. So here I am, stuck between a rock and hard place, because it's either violate my conditions or go back to jail not knowing if we would find someone else to be my surety in time for me to have the baby, not to mention the courts were getting tired of playing this game and I was now on my third surety.

Dakota and I decided we would stay at his brother's house which was close to his aunt's, and that I would just go there at night to sleep and spend my days with his aunt, my surety.

I'm probably about five months pregnant at this time. Other than my living arrangements I was following all the other conditions. I was clean and sober and very excited about the arrival of our son. Things were going as well as they could be for a good three months, until some things happened between Dakota's aunt and Dakota and me, and she, too, decided that she was no longer going to be my surety.

I was eight months pregnant and I knew that if I was going back to jail, I would be having my son there, and the thought of that made me sick. I remember begging and pleading with her to just wait until he was born. Anyway, without getting into details, her decision was to revoke her surety.

I knew I couldn't run from the police being eight months pregnant, and to be honest, I was so sad and devastated that I was starting to give up at this point. I was sick and tired of being on these crazy conditions—mind you, this was two years after I was originally charged with the federal offences. I just wanted it to be over and done with so I could move on with my life. But unfortunately, the justice system is a very slow process and I had no idea when it was finally going to come to an end.

On the 24th of September, 2012, the day before my birthday, I was having some pains in my stomach. We decided I should go to the hospital to make sure everything was okay. Gionni still wasn't due until October 29th. On our way to the hospital, an undercover police officer saw me and decided to stop the vehicle. I was informed that my surety had officially revoked herself and I had to be taken into custody.

Again, I found myself begging and pleading with them not to do this, but because of my conditions there were no other options. Once I got to the police station, I told them that I was having abdominal pain and that I wanted to be taken to the hospital. Within a short period of time, I was at the hospital and being examined by my doctor. He told the police officer that if I continued to have pain, I should be brought back immediately.

After a couple of hours lying in the holding cells at the police station, I was starting to feel worse and again asked to be taken back. The doctor said I needed to be monitored and he was keeping me for observation.

The next morning, I was told by a police officer that I could either stay in the hospital or go to my bail hearing. I figured I should go to my bail hearing and try to get released to avoid having my son while in custody.

The bail hearing went back and forth between the crown, who was not consenting to my release, and my lawyer, who was arguing that an eight-month pregnant woman did not belong in jail, especially not OCDC. He even presented them with a letter from my doctor saying I should be on strict bed rest. I also had an opportunity to plead my case to the judge, and believe me when I say this, I begged and pleaded with her not to send me back to jail, most importantly because I didn't want my son being born while I was in jail.

Now it was time for the judge to make her decision. I remember being full of anxiety listening to what she was saying. She told me she was not granting my bail. My heart literally dropped, but what she said next, I will never forget. "No matter where you go, you'll get the health care you need." To this day, I almost laugh when I think of those words, not because it's funny but because it couldn't have been any further from what really happened to me.

Before I was taken out of the courtroom, I looked over at my mom and Dakota and at this point we were all crying. We all knew that Gionni would be born while I was incarcerated and that was always my biggest fear during my whole pregnancy. Now it was going from being a bad nightmare to a scary reality.

A million emotions went through my mind and it was honestly one of the worst feelings in the world, knowing that my son would now be born in custody, not knowing if Children's Aid would come and take him away because I was incarcerated, knowing that his father would not be there to see his son born. I had absolutely no say in the matter from there on out.

The court officers came to transport me to OCDC and when we got there, they said that I had been in the hospital and that nothing was wrong with me. Neither one of them was even at the hospital with me, and had I not chosen to go for the bail hearing, I could have possibly still been there. But they were ignorant, talking over me and ignoring me, telling the staff at the jail again that I was fine.

After being processed, they brought me to my cell that held two other women around my age. I was pretty depressed at this point and not feeling the best so I really never left my bed. I had been sick throughout my pregnancy where I couldn't hold down much. Apparently, my son was fussy just like his mommy. But I would try to eat as much fruit and whatever I could keep down to make sure my son was healthy.

A couple of days later, the night of the 28th going into the 29th, I had terrible heartburn and I kept throwing up. I was starting to feel very weak. Around 5 am, I threw up in my bed and had to ask the guard on duty to get me new sheets. I didn't sleep much, but I knew Gionni's father was coming to visit me and I was looking forward to that.

I woke up for breakfast but I couldn't eat. I remember one guard telling me that I was obviously a bad mother because I was refusing to eat. She told me that she was going to be making a call to Children's Aid. I had no energy to argue and by this point I was used to hearing ignorant comments from them—not just towards me but other inmates as well.

Around 11 am, they called me out of my cell for my visit and I was still pretty weak. I took my time to walk downstairs to the visiting area. As soon as Dakota saw me he said, "You look really sick, Julie. Your skin's turning grey."

I was having a hard time sitting up. I remember resting my head against the wall and talking to him through the phone because all visits were behind glass and had no contact. After our thirty minutes or something were up, I remember lying on the ground waiting for the guards to unlock the door and bring me back to my cell. I remember telling one of them that I felt really weak and he dismissed it by saying that's what pregnancy does to you. Keep in mind this was my first and only child so I really had no idea what was normal and what was not.

I decided I would just go back to my cell and lie down. Lunch time rolled around but I couldn't eat. One of the guards told me she was bringing me downstairs to see the nurse.

The nurse had me lie down, checked my blood pressure, told me I had heartburn and gave me Tums. No internal examination was done, and she did not check to see the baby's position.

At this point, not only am I weak, but I was starting to get sharp pains in my stomach every couple minutes. But the guards did nothing other than tell me to lie down or that they would let the nurse know. I remember a couple times the other cell mates even knocked at the door to tell them I was pretty sick and that I needed help. The guards never took it seriously.

I later learned that the sharp pains were contractions. I was in labour. I thought I was bleeding at one point and was told it was nothing. Actually, it had been my mucous plug but again this was my first pregnancy—what did I know?

The pains were starting to come closer and were worsening. One guard grew very frustrated with me and told me to lie down and if I couldn't handle it then why did I ever get pregnant.

After supper this guard was so sick of hearing me complain that she told me I was going into a segregation cell. I begged her not to move me. I was getting pretty scared at this point and I did not want to be alone. Not only did she tell me to shut up because I was making too much noise, but she made me carry two mattresses and the rest of my stuff to another cell.

There I was, eight months pregnant, exactly a month away from my due date, and I knew something was very wrong. Another nurse came to see me and demanded that I get out of bed and stand at the door. She asked me what was wrong and told me she would contact the doctor.

Around 6 pm, I felt a gush of water. I banged at the door again to tell them; I was told that I had wet myself. I honestly couldn't get over how ridiculous this was getting. Again I was told to stop whining and to lie down as if I were a dog. Trust me when I say this: Animals are treated better than I was.

The pain was so unbearable. I was banging at door and screaming for help and the other inmates were getting upset that nobody was helping me.

Finally, I inserted my fingers inside myself and I felt something hard. I knew right away it was his foot because I remember feeling his toes. Now I'm beside myself and I'm screaming and the guard comes to the door and has the nerve to ask me if I had a "package." He told me I was being silly, that it was not my son's foot and that it was probably my mucous plug.

I'm literally panicking now because no matter what I said, no matter how loud I screamed, nobody was taking this seriously, and I knew at this point that my son was coming out feet first, which was extremely dangerous for both of us. Had I been in a hospital, I would have had a C-section.

I look down and my son's foot is outside of my body. I'm in full panic mode, screaming for help and banging endlessly on the door. When the guard arrived, I told her to look and I backed away from the door so she could see that this wasn't a joke. I still remember the look on her face, like she couldn't believe what she was seeing, as if I hadn't just been begging for help for the past eight hours.

Within minutes my cell was full of guards and nurses and they had me lying on my bed and telling me not to push, but to anyone who's ever had a baby you know that your body starts pushing on its own. I wasn't even listening to them. I knew my son was suffocating from the way he was being delivered and I just remember lying there for what felt like forever. When is help going to get here? Why isn't an ambulance here yet?

I later found out that for 49 minutes after they came into my cell, nobody called an ambulance.

By the time the paramedics did get there, half of my son's body, both legs and his bum. were out of me and the paramedics told me I needed to push. I think I pushed three times, and my son was born shortly after 9 pm. From a stretcher, I'm asking them if my son's okay. I'm fading in and out, but I'll never forget the fear I felt when they told me they didn't know if he was going to make it. Forget about what just happened. All I was hearing was that my son might die.

You can imagine how hysterical I became. I was fighting to keep my eyes open, and I remember holding him in my arms for the first time and looking at him. He was so perfect. He was everything I ever dreamed he would be and more, and I remember telling him how much I loved him and that I was so sorry for what was happening, but he had to be strong and he had to pull through this. I had no idea that I had lost half the blood in my body or how my health was. I didn't even ask; I didn't even care because I needed to be strong for him and that's all that mattered and that's all that has ever mattered.

As soon as we got to the hospital, we were separated. He was taken to the neo intensive care unit and I was taken into an operating room. I had to be sedated because the placenta was not coming out. It's a little fuzzy for me after that, but I remember coming to and it was about 5 am and I asked the guards if I could call home to tell them that I'd had the baby. Apparently, this wasn't that important because I was told I could wait to call home. Not once did they ask if I was okay, not once did they ask how the baby was. I almost felt like I was dealing with robots because surely no human being with a heart could be that awful even after all they had put me through.

At about 9 am, there was a new shift of guards at the hospital and I was told I could only call my mother. I said, "Hi Mom," and she knew right away something was wrong because I was calling so early, and I told her I'd had the baby. I could hear the panic in her voice, but I was surrounded by staff from the jail and I couldn't really tell her what happened. I had already been told to lie and say

I had my son in the ambulance. She told me that she was getting Dakota and was on her way.

I learned that my son was on a feeding tube and a breathing tube, and he was in rough shape. I kept asking if he was going to be okay; they told me that they really didn't know. I'm not much of a religious person but I've never prayed so hard in my life that my son would be okay.

As I was getting ready to leave my room, a woman walked in and I knew right away that it was a Children's Aid worker. She told me that someone had said that I might be using drugs and that I was in an unhealthy relationship. I told her that both allegations were false. She asked if I was okay with submitting to a drug test and to the baby being tested for drugs, also. I immediately complied. All tests were negative for any drugs for both me and my son. She then said that they would need to speak with Dakota and that turned out to be fine—which I knew, because other than little disagreements, we had no major issues in our relationship.

She wanted to know what the plans were going to be for Gionni until I was released. I had already discussed this with my mom and Dakota once I knew that I was going to be having him while incarcerated. My mother automatically said that she would take Gionni home, and she and Dakota would watch over him until I could.

My mom, Dakota, and I headed to see Gionni after the Children's Aid worker left. It was so awful seeing him in an incubator with all these tubes attached to him. We couldn't hold him or anything but there he was, 5 pounds 9 ounces, with a head full of hair. He was so beautiful and we were so proud. I ended up needing two blood transfusions but, other than that and feeling exhausted, I was physically okay—mentally not so much because on the third day I had to go back to the jail and I had to leave Gionni there, and they still didn't know if he was going to make it.

I can't even begin to describe how I felt leaving him at the hospital. Even though I knew my mom and Dakota would be there with him, I wanted to be there so badly. I kept thinking what if he doesn't make it? Is this going to be the last time I see my son? It truly was awful.

When I got back to the jail, it was business as usual. The same staff who had treated me so badly were working and not one guard apologized. One nurse did apologize. A couple of guards who had come in towards the end of my delivery, and who overall were nicer to the inmates, did ask about the baby but that was literally two of them.

They put me in medical observation for two days, which meant I was in a cell alone until cleared by the doctor from the jail. The last thing I wanted was to be alone, but again, it wasn't an option. Two days later I was back in general population in a cell with two other women. It was really hard being away from Gionni, but it felt good to be able to talk to other people. Now, my main focus was getting out and being the best mom I could be to my little baby.

One day I went to see the worker from the Elizabeth Fry society and I told her what they had done to me. She was disgusted and she told me what they had done was not right at all. At the time I didn't realize the severity of what they had done. I guess you could say I was desensitized. She then put me in contact with the executive director, Bryonie Baxter, who couldn't believe what they had done. She made arrangements to come and see me within a day.

I told her detail after detail. At some point during our conversation, I was asked if I wanted her to contact the media. I never thought at the time that my story would gain as much attention as it has, and to be honest, I was hesitant because I didn't know how long I was going to be in custody and I was scared of the backlash I would possibly get from bringing this kind of attention to the jail.

I thought about it for a few minutes and then I said yes, you can go to the media with my story. She also contacted the ombudsman's office for me, and I started speaking with them on a daily basis. I met two really amazing women from that office who went above and beyond to make sure that I wasn't treated badly and that I was getting phone calls home.

I still remember the first time a guard came to my cell and told me that there were reporters calling the jail to speak with me, and he told me I didn't have to. I kind of got the drift that the guards would prefer it if I didn't, but at this point I didn't care what they wanted. They could do whatever they wanted to me but my son was in a safe place and that's all that mattered.

I was calling home on regular basis and Gionni's health was improving, which alleviated a lot of my stress. Within two weeks he was on his way home, finally. In the meantime, the public and the media were outraged about the treatment we had received and the story was picking up a lot of traction. A wonderful group of women protested outside the Ministry of Corrections with signs saying they needed to reunite me and my son and things of that nature. If any of them are reading this now, I hope they know how thankful I was for that.

My lawyer was making arrangements for an emergency bail hearing because of what had happened, and while that was going on, my first visit with my son since he was born was coming up. At the time I didn't know why, but the jail was on lockdown, which meant my visit was cancelled. I later learned that the men in the jail had found out what had happened to Gionni and me and people were not behaving too kindly towards the guards.

I guess the media were waiting at the gate when my visit was cancelled and, of course, this made the newspapers. So, it was arranged for me to have a special visit outside of visiting hours a couple days later. A few guards made some smart remarks about the "special" privileges I was getting. Yes, they really are that arrogant.

I stood behind glass, so excited to see my son. When Dakota walked in, holding him, I burst into happy tears. Obviously, I wasn't able to hold him but I was so happy to see him. He was the cutest thing ever. I was so grateful that my son was going to be okay, and I was finally getting to see him.

I called home a few times a day to make sure everything was okay with my baby. My mother told me that my lawyer had come to an agreement with the crown attorney. I could be released to the JF Norwood halfway house in Ottawa, and Gionni could live with me. Finally, I was going to be with my son and I couldn't wait.

A dozen reporters were there the day I went to court to be released. I thanked them for getting my story out but I couldn't wait to get back to Ottawa because my mother, Dakota, and Gionni were waiting for me at the halfway house. I remember getting to the halfway house and opening the door to the office and seeing Gionni, asleep in his car seat. I think I actually asked if I could hold him, which was kind of silly since I was his mother. I can't tell you how happy I was to finally have him in my arms. I just started crying.

I agreed to speak with the media and let them see my son and me finally reunited. I still watch that interview a lot. I did that interview because there were so many people supporting us around the world, I figured they'd like to see that all the protesting and all the media coverage really did have a lot to do with my release from jail and my reunion with my son and family!

After the interview I was brought to my private room where I had my own bed and Gionni's crib. Generally, people were two to a room but because I had my son we had our own room. The staff tried to accommodate us as much as possible. Visiting hours were from 7 to 9 pm every night and visits had to be in common rooms of the halfway house.

Residents were not allowed in each other's rooms. I was allowed to have Gionni's father there from morning until 10 pm and he was allowed in my room. This obviously caused some issues with other residents who did not think it was fair, and a few people took it as far as making false complaints to staff and also to Children's Aid.

Obviously, none of these complaints was founded but it did cause some tension.

At this point I was seeing Children's Aid on a weekly basis, voluntarily because it was not court ordered. I also had a nurse from the healthy baby program coming to visit us on a weekly basis so that she could make sure Gionni was meeting all his milestones. He was doing great: strong and healthy and growing bigger and bigger.

The staff helped me a lot. When I needed little breaks, they would watch Gionni. Dakota would drive from Cornwall to Ottawa on almost a daily basis to see us, which really helped because I had pretty bad postpartum depression. At the time, I never dealt with all that I went through because my son needed me, and to me, that was more important than anything, so I put all of that aside and I took care of my son the best way I knew how.

After a couple months of being at the halfway house, I sat down with our Children's Aid worker and I asked her if she had any concerns. She told me that she didn't, so I said that I appreciated everything she had done for us, but that I was ready to open a new chapter in my life and close that one. She then told me that she could understand that, but since there were complaints coming from other residents (who were just doing it out of spite), a new worker would have to come see us every time this happened. It would be in my best interest to keep the file open because she was already aware of everything that had happened. I agreed with her and decided that while I was there, I would continue to let her see us.

I was also recovering from a leg injury. After I was released from OCDC, within two weeks I had an open wound on my leg, and it ended up being MRSA,[1] which I most likely contracted at the jail. I was put on a few different medications. One night I had gotten up to get a bottle for my son. I remember getting really weak, and I passed out. This happened on two different occasions, so I went

---

1   Methicillin-resistant staphylococcus aureus

to the doctor, who informed me that the medication I was on was dropping my blood pressure to a dangerous low and that's why it had that effect on me.

Within two weeks of this incident, I was called out of my room and told that my Children's Aid worker was there to see me. I walked into the room to find a staff member from the halfway house as well as my CAS worker and her supervisor. Right away I got a bad feeling. They told me that I was done parenting at the halfway house and they would be taking my son away from me. I couldn't believe what I was hearing. I started asking questions to which they weren't really responding, and I told them that if Gionni was going anywhere, it would be to my mother since I had signed kinship over to her in the event that I had to go back to jail to finish my sentence. They told me that he would be placed with another family until they had things sorted out.

I was beside myself. No one would even give me a straight answer as to why they were taking him away from me. I thought I'd had a great relationship with my worker; to me it seemed that this was a response to my telling her that I was going to be closing my file with them—because within two weeks she was trying to take my son away from me. As if we hadn't been through enough, now this was happening.

Again I put my feelings aside and knew that I would fight for my son to the end. I informed them that without a court order, my son was not going anywhere. I left the meeting and immediately contacted a family lawyer. I was not going down without a fight. I called home and told them what was going on. My whole family was extremely upset, but we knew we would do whatever it took to stop this from happening.

One day goes by and nothing, then the second day and nothing, and on day three I get a knock at my door and am told that someone is at the door to see me. I came out and I knew right away that they were there for Gionni. CAS was there with a police escort and a warrant to take my son. I started losing my mind.

They gave me a few minutes to get my son dressed and then took him from me.

I broke down. I could not believe this was happening to me. It was unreal. I just wanted to wake up from this nightmare. I set up a meeting with my lawyer and we began the court proceedings to ensure that until this was figured out, I would have visitation with my son at least three times a week. Mind you, Gionni is aboriginal on his father's side, so they were supposed to place the child with a member of the family, and if that couldn't happen, he was to be placed in an aboriginal family. Apart from all of that, papers had been signed stating that he was to go directly to my mother if removed from my care. CAS ignored all of this.

I couldn't believe that after being with my son for only five months, it was coming down to this. One morning I had an appointment to go visit my son at the CAS building, and I was told by the supervisor that she couldn't understand why he had been taken away as I seemed to be a great mother.

Two weeks passed. I came back to the halfway house after a visit with my son and went to take a nap in my room. One of the staff members knocked at my door and told me they needed to speak with me. I said I wasn't in any mood to talk to anyone. I was informed that the police were there and that they were no longer going to let me stay at the halfway house. I began to panic. I was going back to jail.

—

I was petrified at the thought of going back to OCDC as by then people had been fired, reprimanded, and suspended because of what they had done. I called my lawyer from the police station and he made arrangements for me to go to the Quinte jail in Napanee. Once I was there for about a week, my lawyer informed me that I could go to another halfway house in Barrie for six months. I declined and told him I would stay in jail because that way I could come home earlier, and I was willing to do anything I could to get back to my son as quickly as possible. In the meantime, my mom went to court and was awarded temporary custody of Gionni, which took a lot of stress off my back.

The conditions at this jail were like day and night compared to the way things worked at OCDC, and the staff members were cordial and polite to inmates. By this time, Lawrence Greenspon, the lawyer I was using for my lawsuit, had taken over my criminal case as well. He informed me that I only had to stay there a little over two months and I would be back home. It was really hard being away from my son, but I knew we'd be together again soon.

Two and a half months later I'm in court. The judge said that she was comfortable with the time I had in and sentenced me to eighteen months probation. I cried because I knew that part of my life was now over. We set up a meeting with Children's Aid, who agreed I could visit my son as much as I wanted while they asked for a three-month supervision order. Everything was going perfectly. I was with my son every single day and I was so happy to be back with him again. I'll never forget the big smile he had on his face when he saw me and I just held him in my arms for what felt like forever.

—

We were seeing Children's Aid on a regular basis and everything was going fine. Come September, they agreed that they would be giving Gionni back to his father and me so we were slowly integrating him back into my home. I would officially have him back full time October 15th.

Gionni got sick about a week before his first birthday, and I brought him to his doctor who put him on some medication to help him get better. He really didn't seem like his happy self. He was just learning to walk, he had taken his first steps, and he was always furniture walking. His big day came and I threw this huge birthday party for him, but he still wasn't feeling the greatest. We brought him to the hospital and were told he had a cold and he'd get better soon.

Two weeks later, I remember all he wanted to do was cuddle, so I laid him on my chest for a good two hours and held him tight. Gionni was and always will be the love of my life. He meant the whole world to me. I wasn't feeling that great that evening either, so I gave him a big kiss, held him tight, told him I loved him, and then his father put him to bed.

Around 5 am I awoke to Dakota screaming that Gionni was not breathing. I ran to his room and was on the phone with 911. He was completely unresponsive so we both began CPR. I have never felt so helpless in my entire life, but I was trying to keep it together. About three minutes passed and the police showed up and began performing CPR. I remember screaming for help and calling my mom to let her know that Gionni was not breathing.

About four minutes later the fire department showed up and started giving him oxygen. I could not believe this was happening. Six minutes later the ambulance was rushing in and taking him away. The police drove us to the hospital where we were put in the waiting room. I was in complete shock. I remember my mom and Dakota crying and to me it just wasn't registering. I kept asking the nurses what was going on but they couldn't tell me much. Every minute that went by felt like hours.

Finally, the doctor walked in and told us there was nothing else they could do for him. I dropped to my knees and pleaded with him to keep trying—they couldn't just give up on my baby. By now everyone was hysterical and they asked us if we wanted to come and hold him for the last time.

At this point I held my son in my arms and I was just lost. For me, this part is a little blurry. From what I am told I kept saying that it was late and I needed to take him home. It was not registering to me that he was really gone. It was around 8 am by this time and I was told that they had to take him now. I remember kissing him goodbye and not wanting to leave him but I had no choice. I was standing outside of the hospital when they had the nerve to bring my son out in a body bag to be put in the back of a van. I started screaming and I tried to jump inside of the van but one of the police officers pulled me out.

My heart broke a million times that day. How could this be that my son was now gone. After everything that he went through, he should have had his whole life ahead of him.

———

I vaguely recall going back to my mom's; the first couple days are hard for me to remember. Both my sisters-in-law showed up and we ended up back at one of their homes. I don't know how the media got wind of it so fast but they were at the door for hours. We never spoke with them at that time. I was a complete wreck. I remember that nobody would leave us alone. We had family with us at all times. To be completely honest, it's probably a good thing because after Gionni died, I felt like I had no more reason to be alive and that I was going to go be with my son. I no longer saw the point of being here and I think everyone knew that, and that was why they never let me out of their sight.

You know in life when you think of having a baby, you picture yourself buying baby clothes, strollers and toys, but you never imagine picking out coffins, planning funerals, or burying your child. No parent should ever have to lower their child into the ground.

Gionni was my heart and you can't live without your heart. I fell into a horrible depression after my son died. I would find myself at his gravesite just crying and talking to him. Although we had a lot of support from family and friends, I couldn't take living life without him. My life changed forever that day. Every day since has been a struggle. Every night that I go to sleep without him, every morning that I wake up without him is hell.

Losing my son has been the hardest thing that I have ever dealt with. They say it gets easier in time but for me it doesn't. I think you just learn how to cope with it.

———

For the two years following Gionni's death, I was a complete shell of myself. I was using anything from coke to smoking fentanyl patches. Everything was a blur and I stopped caring, even about my appearance. I just lived life in this hell of a bubble in the worst way possible. Then, all of the emotions and feelings I had suppressed from Gionni's death and before welled up and I had a complete mental breakdown. I was crying and screaming and had the worst anxiety attack one could imagine. I remember thinking to myself "you can't keep living like this" so I got help and slowly but surely dropped drugs completely.

I started to speak out and speak up for what I believed in and fought for the changes I wanted to see. It's never too late to take a deep look at yourself and within yourself and want to change, and, like I did, you too can make those changes. It wasn't easy by any sense of the meaning, but it was so worth it.

Often, we tend to judge people—especially those who are incarcerated. But as you can see, especially with my own story, a series of events lead you down a myriad of paths to where you are in this exact moment. Unfortunately, I chose every wrong path and dead end you can imagine. Had you told me at 16 or even 21 that one day I'd be robbing my family to get drugs just to feel normal and that I'd be in and out of jail, I would've laughed in your face. Yet here we are. This should be a cautionary tale at the very least. To the parents reading this, please watch for the signs. I'm not telling you to become a helicopter parent. However, this could happen to anyone's child, even your own. I didn't go from 0 to 100 overnight. Kids are great liars. I was a great liar and my parents had no idea. Your children might fight you on invading their privacy, but

I promise you, they'll get over it. If that means meeting the friends they hang out with and meeting their parents, then you need to. If something feels off, trust your gut, follow your intuition, look through their social media/cell phones. It could make the difference between a "proud parent moment" at graduation or visiting them behind plexiglass. It might seem like a jump, but it's not—I promise you that much.

―

It will be Gionni's 10th birthday September 29th, 2022, and it will be 9 years of hurt, pain and anger since he left this world. Life will never be the same and it's not. Not one day goes by that I don't think of him. He's the last thing I think about before bed and the first thing I think of when I open my eyes. I can proudly say I've been sober going on 8 years with not one slip-up. Withdrawal was also one of the most challenging things I've been through, and if you're an addict, you know how hard it is mentally, emotionally and physically. I've gone on to meet law makers and change makers and spoken at many events. I can honestly say that doing those things has been a huge part of my healing and recovery. I won't say "I'm not that person anymore" because I am. However, I'm the best version of myself now and I'm proud of myself. Don't think it's ever too late to change because it's not. Let this be your sign to go out there and be the best version of YOU.

To my beautiful son Gionni, thank you for guiding me to where I need to be. You are the reason I want to be the best version of myself. You make me want to go and do amazing things, and I know you're as proud of me as I am of you. To my parents, thank you for never turning your back on me no matter how horrible I was. I love you both more than you'll ever know. Dakota, you have been by my side through the worst of the worst and loved me at both my best and my worst. Thank you for everything you do and for blessing me with not only Gionni but my beautiful Dayton, Taylin and Dayani.

Last but not least, thank you to everyone who has supported me through all of this. Bryonie, if it weren't for you, I don't think this story would be the national headline that it was for so many years. Thank you for fighting for Gionni and me when I couldn't. To all the strangers who sent kind messages, letters and even donations, THANK YOU. You'll never know how much it means to me.

There's a star in Heaven…it comes out every night. I know that star is you Gionni—you have come to say goodnight.

Julie Bilotta is a Canadian writer and activist who advocates for change to prison conditions, including policy changes and access to healthcare. After giving birth to her son prematurely at the Ottawa-Carleton Detention Centre in 2012, Julie has litigated as well as advocated for policies to protect the rights of incarcerated pregnant women. Her very personal stories focus on her life experiences and the loss of her son.

Finding Purpose Again

Liz Reeder

Trauma comes in many forms. I was an emergency medical technician and police officer for over twenty years. My first marriage was abusive, and my second was amazing but ended suddenly with the unexpected death of my husband.

Before the death of my husband, I had become disabled and, after his death, I needed to come to terms with the fact that my conditions would only worsen with time. Unfortunately, I had to give up the career that had given me purpose my entire adult life. I have witnessed and experienced trauma that many thankfully never imagine. For me, one of the worst, so far, has been feeling as if I had lost my purpose for being.

In 2016, I found myself very restricted and often confined to the couch or bed, covered in ice packs and braces to help ease pain that was never-ending. I felt useless and worthless which made my health worse. My job had always been to help others and take care of them, and now, I could barely take care of myself.

To help distract myself, I watched a lot of television, which included many shows about the paranormal, unexplained events, and even Bigfoot. That led to me searching the internet for strange things that happened where I lived. What I found was a little surprising.

I lived near Fort Leonard Wood, Missouri, and discovered that there have been quite a few sightings of Bigfoot, especially around a specific trail on the army base. While it was interesting, I tucked that information away in the back of my brain, thinking I would never need to know it again.

That changed two weeks later when the base put out a bulletin saying the trail where the Bigfoot encounters had taken place was closed due to a black bear sighting. I began to laugh. The first thought that popped into my head was, *The army is hiding Bigfoot on the base and claiming it's a bear.* My second thought was, *That needs to be a book.*

Over the next few days, I couldn't stop thinking about my book idea. I had never written anything that wasn't required for school or work. I loved to read and I knew how to write, but it was something that had never interested me up to that point. I knew the process I should follow, which included developing my idea, completing an outline, and developing characters.

However, the thought of trying to do all of that in advance when I wasn't sure what the story would actually be in the end was overwhelming. Instead of trying to slog through all the tedious work that I found distasteful, I simply began telling the story in my head.

I decided on the name of my lead character and began writing. I had no idea where it would go, what would happen, or even the direction the story would take. All I knew was that I had an idea for a book that I would like to read and I needed to put it on paper. As I wrote, I discovered something that became just as important to me as the story I was telling. While I have never been able to journal to express what was happening in my life or mind, I was able to take everything that I felt and give that to my fictional characters.

I was fortunate enough to have a dear friend happily agree to read my book as I wrote it. She gave me the encouragement to not only begin to write the book but to continue writing it at a pace that I later found out was nearly unheard-of. As soon as I would finish a chapter, I would email it to her, and she would give me feedback along with asking when she would get the next chapter because she wanted to know what happened next in the story. Nineteen days after I began writing, my first novel was completed. I had finally found a way to channel everything I was feeling, and I once again felt like I had a purpose in life.

My new purpose was to be a storyteller.

I knew when I had finished writing my first book that the story I was telling was not over. I followed it with four additional novels to complete the series and tell everything that needed to be told about the world I had created and the characters and creatures in it.

I fell in love with writing science fiction, but I also needed other ways to express myself. That led to multiple short stories covering a variety of categories and a novel that fits into both horror and psychological thriller genres. And it turns out that I'm not bad at writing. My first book, which I was told will always be your worst book because you are learning, turned out to be award-winning.

I consider myself to be exceptionally fortunate to have a small group of people who are loyal fans and supporters of my work. They are, in part, what keep me going. When they ask what I am working on or when I will be releasing new work, it reminds me that I am writing not only for myself but for others. That tells me that I am still helping and taking care of others—only in a different way than I had before I became disabled. Some of those supporters have given me ideas for books they wish they could find and read, which I have added to my long and continually growing to-do list since they do not seem to exist yet.

While writing does not change my physical health, it has made a significant change in my mental health. It allows me to refocus when my mind drifts to places it should not. It has taught me that writing fiction can be as therapeutic as journaling and in my case even more so. Most importantly, writing has given me back the ability to feel as though I have value and a purpose. Those are things that everyone should feel they have.

Liz Reeder began writing in 2016 after experiencing the death of her husband, becoming disabled, and leaving her twenty-year career in emergency services. When she had the idea for her first book, 51: The Beginning, *she discovered her love of writing after completing the original manuscript in less than three weeks. Finding that writing fiction helped her cope with chronic pain and depression, she went on to publish the five-book* 51 *series and the stand-alone novel* Wendigo.

Liz continues to write novels and short stories in a wide variety of genres including but not limited to science fiction, horror, thriller, and comedy. She currently lives in the Missouri Ozarks where she was born and finds much of her writing inspiration.

Down for the Ride

Rylie Rockwell

The pressure on my chest grew heavier, pushing me down until I collapsed in the shower under its weight. I was lightheaded, dizzy; it happened again, the static in my brain that I was so accustomed to feeling. Accustomed, but it was a nuisance no less. I sat on the shower floor, staring at my wrists. They were torn open, jagged and bleeding.

Blood trickled down my fingers and washed away with the running water. It burned like fire in my veins as it came rushing out. I wrapped my arms around myself, applying as much pressure as I could to stop the bleeding. To stop the horrible burning sensation. I closed my eyes tightly so that I wouldn't have to look at them anymore. My head spun and I thought I might lose consciousness. Then...

I opened my eyes and unfolded my arms from my torso. I held my hands under the running water. No cuts. No blood. The dizziness had lessened. I took a deep breath and stood up. I finished rinsing the conditioner from my hair and turned the shower off. The pressure on my chest was less now, but the impending cloud of doom still hung over my head, raining its negativity down on my shoulders.

Does this ever get better? Will there ever be more happy days than bad? Or is life just a moving sidewalk that we glide along until we reach the final destination? Will I ever get better, or will my life be this constant cycle of up and down on the emotional roller coaster?

You wanted to know what it was like. You wanted to know how I felt, how aggravated I was in the end…

Kraig's voice rang loud as day in the forefront of my thoughts. *You wanted to know how I felt.* The dizziness snapped away and I was present for that moment. The mental disconnect I had been living with for the past two weeks was gone and it was as if I had been pulled back into my body for the first time since I could remember.

"What are you talking about?" I said out loud. My bathroom was empty. The only sounds came from the traffic outside the open window. Cars passing, music blaring from radios, a truck going over the speed bump left from the construction on the road. No response from him. But my head was clear.

I grabbed my towel and finished drying off and wiped the condensation from the mirror. I bent over the sink and looked at my reflection for a moment. There was no more static in my brain. No more overflowing anxiety from nonstop thoughts. For a moment, there was peace. Silence. Pulling my sweatshirt over my head, I figured I would go up to my room and get some sleep, but I headed towards the front door instead.

I sat on the porch in my rocking chair. I shook a cigarette from my pack and lit up, staring blankly at the cars that drove past my house. The smoke burned the back of my throat and left a chemical taste that made me want to throw up. A month of being smoke-free down the drain—again—all because I could not handle the anxiety.

I looked over at the empty rocking chair next to me. It did not move, even with the soft breeze making its way across the porch. I took a drag and sighed, leaning back.

"You wanted to know how I felt, remember?" Kraig said again. His tone was not condescending. It was not mocking. He was not trying to throw it in my face; he just wanted me to understand. I took another drag and turned again to the empty rocker on my left.

"You're not really here," I said to it. "You're a figment of my imagination. I don't really see you." I knew this was true. He wasn't there, not physically. But in my mind's eye I could see him clear as day, lounged back in the chair, cigarette lit in his right hand. His eyes peered out at the road from behind his glasses, and he smiled. He blew a smoke ring towards the porch roof. I watched it float up and dissipate into the air.

"Right, you're seeing me and hearing me as you remember me. That doesn't make me real, but it also doesn't mean that you're not talking to me. I'm still here, and no matter how much you try to convince yourself you're crazy…you're not." He turned to me and smiled again. "Do you remember, now?"

I did. It was clear as day now. How could I have forgotten? It was early September 2012 when I first noticed the distinctive change in him. I had been gone for two years, living what I thought would be my happily-ever-after in a decent third-floor apartment in Woonsocket. The idea that I thought Woonsocket would be a fairy-tale ending says enough about how disconnected I was, even then. I had dropped out of college, my first long-term relationship had brutally ended, and I had been unable to make ends meet to keep the apartment. No choice but to come back to my childhood home, a disappointment. I was beyond depressed, to say the least.

I was sitting on the bed with Crush, my orange tabby, when the sound of loud bangs, like fireworks, went off outside. Crush jumped up, startled, and bolted under my bed in retreat. I went to the window and looked outside. It was dark, maybe close to 8 p.m. There were no street lamps on the dead-end street. The trees, still full of leaves that had just begun to change, blocked the lights that came from the neighbors' houses. It was completely dark except for the yellow square just a few hundred yards away that came from Kraig's home. His bedroom window was dark; he was in the garage working.

I pulled out my phone and opened up his name in my contacts. "Did you hear that?" I typed out and hit send. I almost did not expect a response, as I seldom got one that early in the evening. Kraig was a night owl, same as me, and was almost always up for a midnight cruise while the rest of the world slept. I had not seen him since I moved home a few months prior. Most nights I spent in my room by myself.

The phone dinged in my hand with an immediate response. "Yeah, the guy out back is shooting again." Ah, gunfire. I snapped a picture of Crush hiding under the bed and sent it back with, "Asshole. He scared my cat."

Another ding. "Oh, are you living back home?"

Alright, so maybe he had not noticed that my car had been in the driveway every day for the past few months. He always had been a space cadet, I laughed to myself. I texted him my response. Then after a moment of thought, added, "If you're not doing anything we should go to the Green Room and get our first 'legal drink'."

I expected him to say no, that he was busy, or that he had plans. Again, to my surprise, he agreed to go out. The condition was that I drove. Strange for him, but no problem for me.

We sat at the almost-empty bar, looking up at whatever sporting event was on the television. I do not think either one of us had any interest in it, but it saved from the discomfort we both felt. I am sure it was not his first time in a barroom, and it certainly was not mine, but something was off.

His Coors Light and my Bud Light sat in front of us, collecting droplets, barely touched. We sipped in silence for a few minutes, and I could not help but notice he was looking around as if he was expecting someone he knew to show up. He looked paranoid.

I took a large gulp of beer and looked at him. "It's expensive as shit here. Would you rather just go grab a bottle of something and drink at your place?"

He smiled and relief came over his face. "Yeah, that sounds good. Just don't get shit-faced like you did when we were drinking that whiskey in your basement a few years ago."

I laughed at him. "Well, we won't buy whiskey then, will we?"

I grabbed a bottle of UV Cake and a bottle of orange soda to mix with it. We sneaked the handle up to his bedroom and plopped down on his sofa. I poured out a couple of drinks and when he took the first sip he almost spit it back out.

"Jesus, is there any soda in this or is it all vodka?"

I laughed and sipped my drink. "So, where's KJ and them? Do you think they wanna come hang out?" I asked, looking at the huge bottle of vodka.

He kinda shrugged. "KJ's not really around anymore. I see him but it's just in and out quick. I've been staying home for the most part."

I suddenly felt sad. I had noticed that his car had not been coming and going as often as it usually did. If he did leave, he was back shortly after. It was impossible not to hear that loud exhaust going down the street at three in the morning, even if I was sleeping. That or the booming stereo bass would wake me up.

I did not press the matter anymore but instead turned to the giant television. It was huge, probably seventy inches, and 1080p HD. It took up the entire wall. Sitting so close to it hurt my eyes.

"Nice TV, but don't you get a headache staring at it all day?" I asked.

He shrugged. "No, I'm used to it. But look over there. See the red dot? It's been like that since I bought it. Drives me nuts."

I looked where he was pointing and did not see anything. I shook my head. He got up, almost knocking over his cup, and indicated the right corner of the screen. I squinted and leaned forward. Sure enough, there was a tiny pixel in the screen that had turned red. It was not noticeable at all until he pointed it out. Even after he took his finger away, I couldn't see it, lost in the other colors of the program.

"Really? You're upset about a tiny dot?" I laughed at him.

His face was stone-cold, serious. "Yeah, I'm thinking about calling the manufacturer for a replacement because it bothers me," he replied.

I rolled my eyes at him and finished chugging my drink. I poured another one, again mostly vodka.

We smoked a couple of cigarettes, and I drank much more than he did. He had some rap music playing through the surround sound, and even though it should have woken me up, I was in a drunken daze just watching him. Kraig was different. Less confident in himself. Less "chillaxed" as I had always referred to him. Something about his body language and the way he was talking made me upset, and I was never morose around him.

The alcohol hit me hard at one point, and the emotions swept over me, warming my sullen vibes and making me feel fuzzy. I wanted to tell him that he could talk to me about whatever he was going through. I wanted to tell him that somewhere deep down I still loved him and that I would always be there for him if he needed me.

I took a deep breath and was going to start spilling my guts (figuratively, not literally) when he turned to me and said, "Do you ever think the brake lights are talking to you?"

His question snapped me out of my drunken love spell and I blinked at him in confusion. "Like on cars?" I asked, dumbfounded.

"Yeah, like…sometimes when I'm driving I see brake lights and I think they're trying to talk to me. They're telling me to stop."

I almost laughed, but then I realized he was serious.

Something was not right. All at once I was hit with a download of various memories from the past three years of random, weird things he'd said to me. Questions and statements that did not make sense. I had always chalked them up as stoner talk, but he hadn't smoked any weed since we'd been back from the bar.

I just shook my head; no, I could not say that the brake lights had ever tried to speak to me. He pulled a prescription bottle out from the cushion of his couch and opened it. He dropped a pill on the table in front of him and began to crush it up. Adderall, I instantly recognized. I thought he had stopped taking it after the incident he had years before.

"Do you want a line?" he asked after he had chopped it. I shook my head and put my hand up. He rolled a dollar from his wallet and sniffed the first line. He looked back at me and said, "Don't fucking say anything about this." I told him I would not. He finished the second line, and we went back to sitting and drinking in silence.

After a few minutes, he said that sometimes he thought the characters on the television talked to him. I started to get scared. The way he was talking reminded me of my grandmother when her Alzheimer's kicked in at an extreme.

"Kraig...are you okay?" I asked. "Is it the pills making you like this?"

He shook his head, looking defeated. "You don't get it. It's okay, no one else does either," he said. I immediately felt horrible for asking and grabbed his hand. He pulled it back. "I just see and hear things sometimes, and I feel like I'm disconnected from reality. It makes it hard for people to be around me, I guess."

I smiled at him, trying to show my empathy. "I don't get it. But if you want to talk to me or need someone, I'll listen to you and I'll be here for you. I'm actually starting school for psychology soon, and maybe I'll be able to understand better once I learn more about different things," I told him. He smiled.

The next two months flew by in a blur. I saw Kraig occasionally for a late-night cigarette or a drive. I had started school again for continuing education in the evenings and spent most of my nights in Woonsocket trying to patch things up with my ex-boyfriend.

When October came around, Kraig seemed to be reaching out more and needing to talk, so I convinced Kyle to stay over at my place whenever he could.

We were lying in bed, close to midnight and almost asleep. My phone went off on the charger, and I sleepily rolled over to pick it up.

The text read, "You around for a butt?" I rolled back to look at Kyle. "Kraig wants me to go smoke a butt. You good?"

"Yeah, go ahead," he said, "but you're supposed to be quitting." He was right. I had not had a cigarette in almost a week. Still, I wasn't going to blow Kraig off. Even though Kyle and I had pushed through and back into a somewhat relationship stage, part of me still held out hope that maybe one day Kraig would see this as more than a friendship. It was probably a pointless hope, after eleven years of being told that he "loved me, but not like that," but hope still.

I walked barefoot through the wet grass and through the bushes to the stone wall in front of my parents' house. I stood by the telephone pole and watched the red glow of a cigarette floating down the street, his silhouette forming as he drew nearer.

"Wasssssuppppp?" He took a drag and the ember lit up his face inside the hood of his jacket. He pulled out a cigarette and handed it to me.

I shrugged, took it from him, and lit up. "Nothin'. What's up with you?"

We sat down on the wall, and he told me how he and his dad were fighting again. It seemed to have become a normal occurrence over the past few months, if not longer. It was strange to him because he had always had a great relationship with his dad when he was growing up. But the more disconnected Kraig felt, the further away his dad seemed.

"But we're gonna go fishing Friday. So hopefully that will be good," he said. I smiled and agreed.

"So, I think I want to go to school to be a funeral director," I said after a short silence. I was expecting an appalled, weirded-out reaction from him. I had not told anyone I wanted to change majors and schools (again) because I didn't think people would understand.

"Like...with dead bodies and stuff?" he asked. I nodded. "That's cool. They make a lot of money, too. Good luck with that. You'll do great." My face lit up and I smiled. Both our cigarettes were out at that point and it was well past one.

"Kyle is sleeping over, so I should go back," I said. We stood from the stone wall and faced each other for a moment. I moved towards him and opened my arms to hug him. To my surprise, he hugged me back. We stayed embraced for a long moment.

"I'm gonna get clean, I promise," he said to me. He let me go and turned to walk back to his house without waiting for my response.

Clean? Clean from what?

The next day I got the same text asking for a cigarette around midnight. I was exhausted from school and just wanted to sleep. I also had been good at not smoking all day and didn't want to ruin it by having the temptation. I texted him back that I was tired and going to bed.

"Tomorrow?"

Yeah, tomorrow was good.

I went to sleep not knowing my world would be turned upside down in less than twenty-four hours.

The ambulance flew up the street first, followed by two town cruisers. Then a third cruiser. I watched out my bedroom window as they pulled into Kraig's driveway and unloaded, marching up to the front door. Kraig's dad let them into the house.

My heart sank in my chest and I grabbed my phone. I dialed his number and listened to the ring on the other end. No answer. I sent a rushed text: "Are you okay???" I waited. No response. Another cruiser had come up the street now, followed closely behind by Kraig's uncle and then his sister. The driveway was full of cars and flashing lights. I pulled away from the window and headed downstairs.

I went outside, looking over my shoulder across the street as I walked to my car. The third cruiser had left, but the ambulance and the other two were still there. I took a deep breath and got into my car. He's fine, I told myself. He has to be fine.

I drove down to Smithfield with intentions to meet a friend from work to go to a party. I had calmed down regarding Kraig and was now faced with social anxiety of having to go out and be around complete strangers.

My phone rang while I was sitting at a traffic light. Kraig's face popped up on the screen above the incoming call button. I smiled in relief and let out the breath I had been subconsciously holding all night. I answered, and my heart sank even further into my gut this time.

"Rylie, it's Donna. Kraig's dead," his mom said on the other end. Everything around me faded out to black. The traffic, the noise from the surrounding cars and trucks, and the lights were all gone.

My grip on the phone tightened and I managed to choke out, "I'm so sorry…what happened?"

"He overdosed…heroin, they think." I couldn't see anything, I couldn't hear anything. I hung up and pulled off Route 44 before the words processed in my brain.

"Kraig's dead. Kraig's dead. Kraig's dead." Donna's words rang in my head over and over.

I punched my steering wheel and screamed. No, this is not real. This is a dream. Some kind of sick joke he's playing on me. This is a prank like that time he told me a paintball was a gumball when we were kids. No, no, no, NO!

I thought I was screaming in my head, but I was screaming out loud. My throat burned and my eyes welled up. My knuckles were red from repeatedly punching the steering wheel. I was dizzy and everything around me was blurry. I realized I had driven a circle three times around a parking lot I didn't remember pulling into. Taking a deep breath, I exited the lot to go back to Route 44.

I sped on the highway, headed back home. "You're not dead!" I wanted to call back to hear him pick up. I wanted to text him and tell him to stop messing around. I wanted him to know that the joke wasn't funny.

The anger quickly turned to paralyzing fear, and I realized it was the truth. It wasn't a joke. I slowed my driving to below the speed limit on the highway and drove in a daze for a couple of miles before I pulled off at a gas station.

I couldn't cry. I was too angry, too numb. I walked into the store, probably looking like a zombie, and grabbed a lighter and a pack of cigarettes. Sat in the car, smoking, and called Kyle. My voice was monotone, dead. He said he would meet me at my house. I pulled out of the gas station and headed home.

The funeral was a week later in town. Kyle agreed to go with me, and I was grateful to have him there to stop me from breaking down in the viewing room. Some people came in and left; some people stayed. Kraig's friends from school and racing all hung out in the back rooms talking, going out for cigarettes every ten minutes.

After the calling hours, there was a short service where a man stood at the front of the viewing room and talked about God and Heaven and the usual bullshit priests say when someone dies. I didn't listen to anything anyone said to me that night, I couldn't hear it. My eyes were glued forward to where Kraig was lying in the casket.

He didn't look like him. He was dressed in his racing suit with a twenty dollar bill folded in his hands from his mom. His glasses were propped up on the bridge of his nose and the funeral director had left his scruffy face be. It was him, but it didn't look like him.

When we went up to the casket to say our final goodbyes, I touched his hand. It was my first time touching a dead body, and I quickly pulled back from it. It was hard and cold like plastic. This was not my best friend; this was a hollow shell.

Kyle and I were the first ones out of the funeral home. I walked to the cool parking lot and felt my knees buckle. I leaned up against him for support and cried for the first time since Kraig had died.

———

Three months later I was driving up 146. It had started to snow. My car was rear-wheel drive and did not have great traction control in any weather, especially icy conditions. The snow had gotten heavy and was sticking to the highway. The other few drivers that were caught out with me had slowed to below fifty miles per hour as they made their way around the bend just past the Purgatory Chasm exit. I had also slowed to not "glide" as Donna called it.

"How could it have gotten that bad?" I said to the empty passenger seat beside me. "You were struggling. You were having a hard time. But you were NEVER the type to give up."

There was no answer.

I was exhausted, physically and mentally. The last three months I'd spent in bed, only leaving my room to go to the bathroom or get food from the kitchen. I had cut off communication with everyone.

This was my first real dance with grief. Me, a girl who was fascinated by death her entire life, and obsessed with the paranormal and possibility of an afterlife, had been defeated by the silence that came from the empty chair that I was left with.

"If you won't talk to me, can you show me?" I asked quietly. A song came on the car radio. It was the one I had played on repeat for the weeks following Kraig's funeral. Normally, it calmed me and brought me a sense of peace. That song was his way of letting me know he was okay.

When it came on that time though, it brought out rage. Anger like I had not felt since the night he died. There was still silence from the passenger's seat. Silence in my head. No answer from the other side.

"Fucking let me feel what you felt!" I screamed. My foot pressed on the gas and I found myself passing the other cars on the highway. The speedometer read seventy-five now. "Just let me fucking get a glimpse of what went through your mind! What the fuck was so bad that you got to this point!"

Eighty-five now. It was completely white-out conditions in the middle of the day. I couldn't see in front of me. I didn't care. I knew there was a bridge overpass coming up. If I hit it, fuck it. Anger was flowing through my whole body now, pressing down on the gas.

There were no answers, no closure. No more 3 a.m. car rides and conversations that I would have to spend the next two weeks trying to decipher. No more strange questions or statements that left me perplexed. It was all gone, and I was tired of fighting my own feelings. I was tired of feeling numb. My thoughts raced in a whirlwind and I couldn't see the road in front of me. I stopped looking at the speedometer. I knew the overpass would be in front of me soon...just a little farther.

"FUCKING SLOW DOWN!"

The words hit me in the front of my head like a baseball and knocked me back in my seat. All the thoughts stopped spinning and dropped. They exploded on the floor of my mind and shattered, finally still.

My foot came off the gas, and I slowed down just as I came around to the overpass. My entire body was tingling as the anger faded and I was left in shock, like a toddler who had just been disciplined by their parents for the first time. I took the next exit and got off the highway to turn around and head back home.

The memory came and went in the blink of an eye, and I was staring out at the traffic on my front porch again.

"I begged to feel the way you felt," I whispered to the empty rocking chair next to me. "I wanted so badly just to experience the things you did before you died. So I could understand…"

He nodded and took a drag from his cigarette.

"I created this reality in my head. I put myself in this position… seven fucking years later…and didn't even realize what or why I was doing it." Another nod of agreement. "This is a living hell. How do people function like this? How does anyone go throughout their day with static in their brain and nonstop thoughts? The out-of-body experience is enough to make anyone want…"

"It's enough to make someone desperate to do anything to shut it off," he finished for me.

"How do I shut it off? I wasn't like this before. Anxiety, yes. Bipolar, yes. But I was never so trapped in my own brain that I was seeing things. I don't want to feel like this anymore," I started to cry. "I get it now, so now make it go away. I know I asked for this, but please, make it go away."

He smiled gently at me and stood up from his seat. "What did you do that turned it on?" And he and the static were gone.

◦━◦

Rylie Rockwell is a mother, author, and graduate from Mount Ida College in Newton, Massachusetts, with a degree in Funeral Services. Diagnosed with bipolar disorder in her early 20s, Rylie is an advocate for mental health awareness and ending the stigma surrounding those diagnosed with mental illnesses. She has had a love for creative writing since she was a child and continues to use it as a coping mechanism in her day-to-day life. Her short story "Down for the Ride" is her first published work and captures a brief moment of what an anxiety attack can look like for someone suffering from a bipolar disorder. She hopes that, by sharing her story with the world, more people who are suffering will come forward and seek help, realizing they are not alone.

THROUGH IT ALL

Catherine Athieno

It was the 12th of January 2009 when my mum passed away because of HIV syndrome, a traumatizing moment in life that will remain at the back of my memory for decades. Mom had accepted to adhere to her HIV treatment faithfully but she was tormented when people started condemning, segregating and judging her. This negated her zeal to live longer because she felt guilty instead of focusing on getting better. I live in Uganda and I come from a family of eight children, two of whom were adopted by Mum when her younger sister passed in 2000. When we lost Mum, life started darkening for us, and my dream to become a medical doctor ceased.

My father was a businessman who dealt in timber while Mum had a restaurant. Mummy's occupation earned a daily income that met the day-to-day demands of the family. Dad made sales once in a while and supported the family mostly by paying our school tuition and the rent on our house.

But after Mummy's death, Daddy's income alone was not enough to cover education, clothes, food, and other basic needs. He tried to run other businesses like purchasing food in villages, where extensive farming is done, and selling it in towns to places like restaurants. But he was inexperienced, and with the added trouble of sudden price fluctuations and goods perishing, the business collapsed. Dad became financially incapacitated.

Our relatives became concerned about us, knowing that Daddy was struggling to take care of all his children. They decided to divide us among themselves to relieve him from the overwhelming responsibility.

My father was drained and most of the time he was depressed. A family that was once living happily together was split up. Dad relocated to his home village from which he later disappeared, gone off to some unknown place—probably to reset his life. His absence tortured us the more as at some point we thought he could have poisoned himself. We were so lonely and psychologically tormented. All of our house belongings were divided as each relative picked whatever they loved, and we children were left with nothing.

While we were living at different places with our relatives, life became harder. We seemed to be burdens when it came to meeting our needs. We had to endure segregation, loneliness, and missing school some days because of heavy workloads. At times, we sought work like washing clothes for people and fetching water from far places for restaurant owners just to earn some money to feed ourselves.

It was at this point that my younger sister, Claris, decided to travel to Dubai in the United Arab Emirates to find work as a housemaid. But life didn't work out for her while in Dubai. She found her way back home to Uganda after enduring sexual harassment by her boss's son as well as the unbecoming behavior of the Arabs.

In fact, one of her friends—an Ethiopian housemaid—died after her boss tortured her for days with a hot flat iron. This tragedy traumatized my sister, causing severe depression that took her years to heal from after she had returned home.

At age seventeen, I received Jesus Christ as my only Lord and Saviour while I was serving the Lord in the church. God through His unfailing love brought a loving man to me. Robert proposed and promised to further me in my education. He met my relatives and we had a simple wedding. He faithfully saw me back to school for my nursing course. After two and a half years I attained a certificate as an Enrolled (certificate) Nurse which is an entry level professional, but this programme will be phased out soon so my practicing licence will be terminated. Soon, I will go back to finish my degree and qualify to be a Registered Nurse. This will put me in a better position to support my four siblings.

I birthed my first born in 2011 and conceived my second in 2015. Everyone in my new family was in sound health. However, whilst pregnant for my second child, I noticed that my youngest sister Luckshim, who was eight years old, started falling sick repeatedly as well as losing significant weight. I decided to take her to a better hospital for further examination. It was at this point that I received the news that she tested positive for HIV. In denial, I started panicking. The sad memories I went through when hospitalising my mother regenerated and I mourned her afresh as though she had just died. At that time, my husband was travelling for work where he spent two weeks before returning home. I went into severe depression for over a week. Suddenly I could no longer sense fetal movements of my unborn eighth month baby. I rushed to the hospital and an abdominal ultrasound scan could not detect the fetal heartbeat of my baby at all. After a while, the unborn was pronounced dead (stillbirth). Procedures were done to see that my life was saved at the same time that burial arrangements for my baby were being made. Following my baby's death, I spent days and nights as though I had lost a part of myself on earth. My senses were numb and I couldn't function anymore. My face was continuously bathed with tears and much more trouble than before, but through the prayers of God's saints, I recovered.

I have worked hard to convince my youngest sister Luckshim to adhere to treatment but sometimes she resists. She always demands to know why she should be the one to bear the burden of taking antiretrovirals (ARVs) when she is innocent. Up-to-date on her medications, she feels unfortunate and stigmatized. Her situation is terrible but she also knows, if she wants to stay healthy, she needs to be consistent with her medication.

After this storm, in 2016 I received a phone call from an aunt that one of my cousins, Celine, who had been adopted by Mum, will not go to school anymore because of lack of tuition money. At the age of sixteen, men took advantage of her. She conceived and contracted HIV. My spirit felt so weary and I waivered in faith to a point that I nearly committed suicide. Robert suspended his job and had to stay home full-time to support me going through my recovery. Currently, Celine lives as a single mother of an eight-year-old girl. At times, Celine has self-sabotaged, but I work hard to counsel her so that she takes her HIV treatment and stays healthy.

My four sisters and brother left school because of no funds for tuition, but I am glad I am now able to support two of them in high school.

Robert is such a kind husband who always welcomes my sisters and brothers in our home. He supports me by parenting my siblings through counseling, praying, and encouraging them in times of challenges. We are also now blessed with two boys and one girl—Joshua, Jether, and Jinah.

The journey of our life has been filled with tears and agony, but we are healing from our past trauma. God is indeed taking care of us now.

My elder brother and I hold fast to God's promise in Psalms 27:10 to care for orphans. Therefore, when God blesses us financially, we hope to open a technical school in order to empower young people who have dropped out of school with skills and an orphanage home to raise many more hopeless children and to preach Christ in order to win more souls in the kingdom (Proverbs 31:8-9). To God be the Glory!

When my father and my mother forsake me, then the LORD *will take me up.* (Psalms 27:10, KJV)

⌒ ⌒

Catherine Athieno is married with three children. She lives in Uganda where she works as a nurse. She is truly excited to be included in

Women Write Now: Women in Trauma, *an anthology of personal stories of trauma and recovery from women around the world. Her story is intended to assure orphans that a Journey with God is a path to glory regardless of all storms of life after the loss of a parent(s). She welcomes anyone to reach out to her and can be reached at* cathyathieno81@gmail.com.

You Might Eat Organic, but You're Still Full of Baloney

Alia Luria

My aunt, you know, the former chief, says that they probably served you a white bread sandwich for dinner and maybe some powdered eggs for breakfast. She speculated that it probably had two pitiful scraps of nutritionally devoid bologna between the stale, tasteless slices. Subsistence fare. I hope you looked at that sandwich, in all its over-processed, non-organic, carbohydrate-filled glory and regretted every decision that brought you to it. You probably didn't eat it. It didn't come from Whole Foods.

Still, I know regret is a lot to hope for. I looked at your mug shot today when I had to circulate it around the office for notice purposes. Thanks for that, by the way. It's always been a personal goal to explain to my co-workers that my entire weekend was a stress-fest of dealing with your mistakes and why. You didn't look contrite to me. Your brown eyes stared straight into the camera like it was a Sears Portrait Studio shoot, and your lips had that slight curl, that sarcastic non-smile that graces your face in most photos. You didn't appear overly bothered that you were being booked into jail for stalking.

Perhaps in your mind, I was completely unreasonable for reporting the hand-written note left in my mailbox while I wasn't home, a note that came four months after I asked you never to contact me again. In the fairytale to which you are central, you're entitled to my time and consideration, even though I ended it between us in January. I can only imagine the dumbfounded look Officer Kim bestowed you when you told him that you just wanted to see if I'd respond. After all, Officer Kim read that text from February where I outright told you that I had called the police and that you needed to leave me alone or it would escalate. It was blunt. It was unequivocal. It should have been the end.

Then again, you did think I was pathetic for calling the police that evening. That was a nice touch for the judge. I'm sure when he ordered probable cause for arrest with no objection or discussion from the public defender, he noticed the gaslighting, the guilt-tripping, and the projection in those series of responses, and it all was crystal clear to him even if not to you. I didn't even look at you to see your reaction. I kept my eyes focused on the judge. My mom and aunt watched the bail hearing on the public livestream. My aunt said you were stoic and maybe compliant. My mom thought you looked a little cocky. I'm inclined to believe Mom. Jail can't get you down! You're indomitable!

But I meant what I said when I told the judge I bore no animus toward you. I have not rejected communication with you because I'm hurt or spiteful. It's because no amount of discussion will make you understand your fundamental lack of respect for me. I don't hate you. I just don't have time for you. Find someone else to teach you how to be a considerate person. Or don't. I don't care.

You probably still think that I was intolerant of your alternate lifestyle, but our time was already coming to an end. Your unspoken decision to be polyamorous—you know, the one you didn't mention until after you had slept with your ex-girlfriend on New Year's Eve— was not the reason we aren't together anymore. I was content to let you think that at the time, since it was as good a reason as any to break up. Certainly, having intimate relations with Tiffani put a nail in that coffin, but it doesn't seem to have occurred to you that me not caring to spend New Year's Eve with my boyfriend is the coffin. Tiffani is just a nail. Her untreated herpes is just another nail. Your need to lie about it is a nail, too. And your tearful entreaty that you loved both of us is just the lacquer on the box.

Salute that box, stick it in the earth, and sprinkle the ground liberally with salt. Nothing will grow from that wreckage, buried in the depth of your blindness. I don't think you noticed that I didn't cry as I ushered you out of my house and my life the night you buried us. If you had just seen me, you would not have spent the night in jail.

Yes, you probably think. *If Alia had seen me instead of ignoring me, this wouldn't be happening. She did this to me.*

But you are wrong. If you had seen the woman I am when we were still together, not the short, small woman with a fine-boned and freckled face, but the *me* under the slight exterior, you would not have put yourself in jail over this. You would not have given yourself a criminal record. You would not have suffered that bologna sandwich or those powdered eggs. I may be anxious, but I am not weak-willed and soft. I may be open, but I am not a doormat to wipe your feet on. I may look small on the outside, but I am strong. Also, I'm a lawyer. And maybe you shouldn't have screwed with a lawyer. We keep detailed written records. We document. Our whetstone is preparation. Our words or lack thereof are our blades.

You should not have texted fourteen times to no response, not called twice to be ignored, not showed up at my house uninvited, not contacted me on Facebook messenger to be blocked, and not sent me two cents on Venmo. That was an amusing birthday present, by the way. Two cents the day after my 40th birthday, a birthday I was so looking forward to. I almost didn't block you just to see if you would keep it up. Maybe I could eventually have gotten a latte from your random blathering.

Finally, you should not have left that hand-written note in my mailbox on Friday night telling me to meet you for coffee on Sunday with your name and phone number included. It should not require a judge and a no contact order for you to understand that I am uninterested in friendship, uninterested in your emotional baggage, uninterested in being in your menagerie (look it up if you've forgotten what it means) of ex-girlfriends with whom you routinely socialize. Say hi to them for me! I'm sure you will tell them in detail about what a horrible person I am. After all, you told me how crazy they all are, even though you still meet them for dinner or to hang out. Come to think of it, they are all probably lovely women.

Some movies and novels praise the persistent lover who never gives up. He is the hero. He gets the girl. She realizes how much she loves him and how she could never have been happy or complete or fulfilled (yada yada yada) without him. He was there all along in his awkward but angelic perfection waiting for his moment of glory. But we do not live in the fantasies of writers and directors. We live in the real world. In the real world, I said, "I do not want to speak to you or maintain any contact. Please stop texting, calling, messaging, and do not come to my house. You are not welcome on my property." If it sounded wooden and formal when you read it to yourself, it was. Three cops helped me write it while we all stood around my living room. After that, they asked me a bunch of personal questions about our sex life. Yes, I did tell them about that one time that thing happened. It seemed relevant. Best night ever.

You are not John Cusack with a boom box in the rain. You are not Tony Robbins psyching yourself up to reach your goal at any cost. I will admit that I haven't consulted Tony directly, but I don't think he would have been on board with your plan to get arrested for stalking. In any case, that is not how this works. I am the one with agency over my mind and my body. I choose who belongs in my life and who does not. I am the one who decided not to respond to you. You are the one who decided that "No" means keep trying. You are the one who decided that the pursuit of the dead and buried was worth a night in jail.

You are not the love of my life. You are not the one who got away. You didn't break my heart. You are not even the bane of my existence. You are just a guy who had to spend the night in jail and probably stare at a disgusting bologna sandwich until you discarded it, all to hear from a judge what I already told you. Leave me alone.

❧ ～ ❧

Alia Luria lives in Temple Terrace, Florida, with her two Pembroke Welsh Corgis, Ein and Cookie. When she's not busy writing her epic sci-fiction/fantasy series or otherwise noodling on new ideas, she is very, very busy practicing business and technology law and serving as the Director of Anthologies for Something Or Other Publishing. Apart from writing and reading voraciously, she really enjoys knitting, painting, travel, and photography, and mixing them together.

She holds a Masters in Fine Arts in Creative Writing Fiction from Fairleigh Dickinson University and has had short pieces published with Toho Journal, Wingless Dreamer, *and* Northwest Review. *Her* Artifacts of Lumin *series was recently acquired by Something Or Other Publishing and will be re-released in wider distribution through their channels.*

You can learn more about Alia at her website, alialuria.com, or by following her on Instagram @alialuria.

You Might Eat Organic, But You're Still Full of Baloney *was originally published in the Winter 2020 edition of* Northwest Review *and is printed with permission.*

OKAY

Ashlyn Inman

"Oh please, as if you've ever experienced trauma in your life."
A held breath for one moment too much, a hesitation for
one beat too long, and I knew the curtain had fallen.

"You haven't, have you?"

I fixed my eyes on the granite countertops and willed the tears to go
back. I knew that the longer I waited to respond, the more I condemned
myself; but I also knew that the moment I looked into her eyes I'd be
through anyways. All of the words I had ever learned vanished from my
vocabulary, and I was left grunting "uhhhh" like a child or a caveman.

Mothers were supposed to protect their children, and here I was
trying to protect my mother.

"Ash?" she whispered softly.

They tell you about fight or flight, but I had only recently
learned about the third option: freeze. And here I was again, voice
caught in my throat, freezing.

"I—" How do you begin this conversation with someone who still
thinks you're a virgin? "Something happened when I was in London."

Apparently, you begin by being vague.

—

"I want to suck some British dick," I announced to my friends.
"I said that I would have a one-night stand before we went home
and it's our last night, so the clock is ticking."

Emily tried not to show her disapproval. We were out in London for a summer program for musical theater, and between workshops and outings with friends, I hadn't had much time to flirt with British bachelors. But there was a boy who was in the school to study Shakespeare who had caught my attention from day one. We had said a few words to each other in passing, but most of our interactions came from intense eye contact here and there. And as a fan of *Pride and Prejudice*, this was all the indication I needed to know he was interested in me.

We were on our way to a pub to celebrate the end of the program. The only reason Emily even agreed to come out with us instead of FaceTiming her girlfriend was because our friend Courtney was leaving early the next morning.

The bar was crowded with college actors from various countries. I got myself a cider and began scanning for my target.

There he was. Beautiful, blue-green eyes, thick lips sipping a pint. I slid through the crowd, making my way over to him.

I don't remember how the conversation began, or what we said as we flirted, but I remember the press of his hand on the small of my back, pulling me in closer to him so I didn't get lost in the sea of people.

There was a party some of the students were going to, and he asked me if I was going. A sharp look from Emily prompted me to say no, I have to help my friend pack. I said maybe he could come over later after the party, and he said for sure and gave me his number on WhatsApp.

We parted ways and I was sure that was the end of that.

The next morning, I walked down the hall, turned the corner, and quietly rapped on Room B. Emily sleepily opened the door, and her eyes widened when she saw me up two hours before we needed to leave. I'm usually the type of person to roll out of bed and shove stuff in a suitcase mere minutes before we took off somewhere.

"Ash? What's up?"

I found it hard to hold eye contact with my best friend of three years. "I, uh, I have to run down to the pharmacy really quick." She opened her mouth to interrupt me, but I pressed on. "I'll explain later. Just don't tell Kailey." (Kailey was the other girl we were traveling with.)

"Are you okay?" she asked as she studied my downcast face.

"Yeah, I'm fine. I just have to take care of something." I gave her a tense smile and she smiled softly back, which was her silent agreement to keep my secret.

I walked down the hall, pausing momentarily in my room to grab my purse. As I clambered down the stairs of the dorm building, I counted out the pounds I still had and wondered if the British pharmacy would accept my American credit card.

The gray streets were crowded with people walking to work. Men in navy suits barked at people on the other end of their cell phones. Women in jewel-tone blouses and khakis tapped on their phones while teetering along on shiny heels, clutching their tote bags under their elbows.

I navigated the two blocks to the pharmacy and walked through the automatic doors, through the aisle that had alcohol on one side and snack packs on the other, all the way to the back counter.

A tall, stout man with a five o'clock shadow stepped forward when I made it to the counter. "What can I help you with, ma'am?"

I stared at the counter and picked at my right pointer fingernail. "I need Plan B. Or the morning after pill. I don't...whatever you call it."

The man pulled his lips into a flat line as he turned around. "The generic or branded?"

"Just generic," I muttered.

He grabbed a purple-blue box off the second shelf from the top. He turned back around and set it on the counter. "Ma'am, there are some questions I have to ask you before I sell it to you."

I shifted my weight to my other leg and nodded.

"Do you understand that this pill is a form of birth control, but it is not guaranteed to prevent pregnancy?"

"Yes."

"Do you understand the side effects can include nausea, vomiting, bleeding, and light-headedness?"

"Yes."

"Is this your first time taking this pill?"

"No," I admitted.

He clearly wasn't expecting this answer. But he continued, "Okay, have you had to take this drug within the last three months?"

I paused. "Yes," I whispered.

"When?"

"A month and a half ago," I murmured.

He stared at me incredulously. "What are you thinking? This isn't supposed to be something you use regularly! You could really damage your body! How could you be so careless?"

My voice caught in my throat as tears welled up in my eyes. I bit my lip and stared at the floor. My tears turned the tile into a kaleidoscope of grays and yellows.

This man I never met before immediately realized he had overstepped. "Thirty-eight pounds, ma'am," he said quickly. I swiped my card through the machine while he put the box in a brown paper bag. Turns out they did take American credit. As soon as the receipt printed, I snatched the brown bag and made my way back to the dorm building.

The room seemed smaller this morning with my suitcases packed and ready to go. I tore open the box and pulled out the tiny pill. My hands shook as I grabbed my water bottle and swallowed the pill down.

A few hours later we sat on a train and Emily watched me carefully as I tried not to throw up. Kailey, oblivious to the world, chatted about the party Emily and I had passed up the night before.

The next few months were characterized by binge drinking and kissing as many boys as I could—even fucking a few of them—to prove that I was confident in my sexuality. I bragged about the beautiful man I slept with in London.

—

Six months after we got back from London, I was sitting on Emily's couch in her apartment. She was in a cream-colored chair perpendicular to me with her girlfriend Maggie sitting on the floor in between Em's legs. As Em played with Maggie's short hair, Em and I shared London stories. Maggie asked about the guy I was with in London.

"Well." I laughed and told the story up to the point where the guy and I parted ways. "We had just said goodbye to our friend Courtney and gotten back to the dorm. I took off my makeup and threw on an old sorority t-shirt and soccer shorts. I was about to get into bed when my WhatsApp buzzed. His name was Corey, and there was a message from him saying he was on his way back over and if I was still awake. So I said I was, and when he arrived, I snuck him upstairs to my room. We started kissing, and he took my top off and pushed me down on my bed, and I propped myself up to undo his pants. And good Lord, was he big. Uncut, but big."

Emily winced and I realized I didn't need to go into that much detail. I coughed. "Anyways. We were kissing and he pulled down my shorts, and that's when I asked if he had a condom. And he said no, and I said that I was sorry, but I don't have sex without a condom but that we could do everything else. And uh," I faltered, "and then he kinda pushed himself inside of me, and I wasn't really sure what to do, so I kinda just laid there and then I asked him to just not come inside me, but he grunted and I realized it was too late. And so we sat around for a bit and he went home. And the next morning I went to a pharmacy and got Plan B and we never spoke again."

Maggie stared at me with her mouth hanging open. She laughed in the dry way she did when she was uncomfortable. She looked back at Emily briefly and turned back toward me.

"That…like, wasn't okay. You know that, right?"

"I…" I didn't know what to say.

What I didn't tell them about was how I frantically shoved two fingers up my vagina and clawed out his cum from inside me. I didn't tell them how I pulled my shirt back on to hide my vulnerable, naked body and sat on the bed and suggested he should leave. I didn't tell them how he sat down in the chair at the desk across from my bed and didn't leave. I didn't tell them about the way he sighed and sputtered and tried to explain himself. I didn't tell them how I begged him to leave and he refused. I didn't tell them how he crept back over to where I was on the bed and cornered me against the wall and slid his thick hand up between my thighs until my body quivered and shook and betrayed my emotions. I didn't tell them that after that, he finally left, and I never felt more alone.

—

Until Maggie said that what happened wasn't okay, I hadn't allowed myself to think about the "r" word. Because I couldn't cope with it being non-consensual.

Because rape is. Rape is screaming, not staying silent. Rape is struggling while you're being held down, not lying still. Rape is in alleyways or at frat parties, not in a room you let the man into. Rape is what happens in stories and movies and plays where you can objectively observe if "the rape scene" was believable, not what happens to you.

—

It was another few months before the man I'd fall in love with would hold me as I told him the full story of what happened in London.

A few more until I finally unpacked the event with a therapist. A few more until I stopped using alcohol to fill the hole left behind. And a few more until I finally gave my parents the abridged version.

———

After my mom asked me about the trauma in my life, I sat down my parents and told them that what happened in London hadn't been my first time, but that it had happened.

I hadn't told my parents at first because I refused to let myself believe I had been raped, and later because I was afraid my parents would judge me.

I had made a bad decision. But I took away my consent. Just because I froze does not mean I gave my consent. Just because I didn't fight back does not mean I gave my consent. Just because I let him in does not mean it was any less of a rape when he forced himself inside me.

What I didn't anticipate was how I could accept that fact but question every decision I made after that night. There are days I can't even choose what restaurant I want to eat at because I'm afraid of making the wrong call.

Is that relevant?

Maybe not.

But it's the last part of the hole I need to fill. I've accepted that it wasn't my fault and filled the emptiness with love. I've forgiven myself so many times, but I still have to forgive myself all over again every now and then.

I don't know how to close this out because I still live with my trauma every day. The dull ache hasn't gone away, so how do you finish a story that's still being written?

I've imagined a million different scenarios where I change the ending of that story—where I don't text back and pretend I had gone to sleep, or where I screamed and woke the entire flat up. I've imagined returning to that pharmacist and telling him that I wasn't the kind of person who used Plan B as birth control. I had birth control, and the first time I had to take the pill was because of an accidental condom break. I've imagined a world where I never thought I was the one who fucked up.

And I've imagined how long I would have gone on self-medicating in denial if Maggie hadn't said, "That wasn't okay."

———

Ashlyn Inman is currently working towards a Master of Fine Arts in Creative Writing at Fairleigh Dickinson University. She received a Bachelor of Fine Arts in Musical Theater at Coastal Carolina University and currently lives in Nashville, Tennessee. She's eternally grateful to Alia Luria and the entire SOOP team for the chance to share her story, and she wouldn't be where she is today without the support of her parents and partner, Noah. Follow her at @ashwednesdays on Instagram to see what she's doing when she's not watching Star Wars. *www.ashlyneinman.com*

SELECTED POEMS FROM GATHERING BROKEN LIGHT

Heather Lang-Cassera

Salt-cracked faces,
humming to the fire.

The morning borrows the land behind us.

Gathering broken
light, we no longer drift
over the sun.

*The following poem was composed of lines from an
article in* The Washington Post *by Alex Horton, "The
Las Vegas shooter modified a dozen rifles to shoot like
automatic weapons."*

In a frantic nine-minute window of intermittent gunfire
the barrels can reach several hundred degrees.
Components used together in a weapon suggest a desire

to shoot large amounts of automatic-like fire,
turning orange & even blue as rounds travel thousands of feet,
in a frantic nine-minute window of intermittent gunfire.

Nevada Law allows the purchase of machine guns & silencers,
a meticulous collection of accessories.
Components used together in a weapon suggest a desire.

An AR-15 type rifle with a bump or slide fire
(automatic weapons used by the military have lever releases)
in a frantic nine-minute window of intermittent gunfire

bounce, or bump, the weapon into the trigger finger.
The bump fire mechanism includes a high capacity.
Components used together in a weapon suggest a desire,

which helps the shooter acquire...
Regulate the side of high-capacity magazines.
In a frantic nine-minute window of intermittent gunfire
components used together in a weapon suggest a desire.

I cannot help but wonder
which never-learned lullabies
could have best passed

each of those nine minutes.

In an alphabet of grief—

a buildable city

dipped endlessly

fireflies gave heed

illuminated jars kept lonely

marigolds nodded overlooking pasts

quietly resisting stoicism

trembling unstoppable…

I called my mother's dry voice desert
years before I knew the beauty
of the Mojave. Perhaps
This was patience. Maybe
this was becoming.
Here, staccato
cacti wait. I
beg,

    sing.

Heather Lang-Cassera is a Clark County, Nevada Poet Laureate Emeritus (2019-2021); a 2022 Nevada Arts Council Literary Arts Fellow; a publisher and editor for Tolsun Books; and a lecturer with Nevada State College where she teaches College Success, Creative Writing, Professional Editing and Publishing, and more. Her book, Gathering Broken Light (Unsolicited Press, 2021), a collection of poems, was written with the support of a Nevada Arts Council Project Grant and was recently named the 2022 NYC Big Book Award Winner in the category of Poetry—Social/Political. Learn more about the author at heatherlang.cassera.net.

    These poems are excerpted from Gathering Broken Light and are used with permission and available for purchase at unsolicitedpress.com. *All royalties go to the Vegas Strong Resiliency Center.*

Becoming Me – From Vulnerability and Fear to Strength and Resilience

Jenny Rortvedt

October 3rd, 2015. Almost five years. Five years since one of the worst days of my life. Nearly five hours of torture.

It was 9:53 p.m. I was locking up the house to go to bed. I heard a knock at the door. I peeked out my side window to see HIM. Immediately, I remembered how he once told me that he can get anyone to do anything if he can look them in the eyes. I should not have opened the door, but I did.

We talked. For the hundredth time, we talked. Beating a dead horse, as my mom would say because it was long over between us. He wanted to "show" me he loved me. I remember focusing on the stars out of my living room window as he had his way with my body. That is all he could have of me, and I was praying he would be done soon.

He realized he was getting no reaction from me, so he stopped. This made him angry, though. For the first time in three years, I was finished with him, and he knew it. He had always seen me as weak, like I was when we first met, but maybe he understood I wasn't that way anymore.

He left. Thank God.

I thought I was done with him.

A few minutes later, when I was in bed, I heard a bang. My tormentor was back, and he was kicking down my front door. I don't know why I ran to my door instead of reaching for my phone, but I did.

He needed his crack, and he needed my money to get his crack. He had already taken so much from me in those three years— thousands and thousands of dollars that I would never see again— and I refused to give him what little I had left. I was being stubborn. It was just money, but he manipulated and stole so much from me that I didn't want to give him anymore.

At some point, he turned his back, so I reached for my phone to call 911. He was able to get it from me, quicker than I could dial. I still have the hole in my wall where he threw it. Now, what do I do? I ran for the stick that was in the tracks of my patio door. I swung it at him, but it broke on his forearm and the pieces flew in different directions.

It didn't faze him.

I fell to my knees with him over me, threatening to hit me with one of the broken pieces. But then, he grabbed me by my biceps and picked me up. He squeezed so hard that it brought tears to my eyes. I blinked them back so he didn't have the sight of me breaking to excite him further. I couldn't help the whimpers that escaped as he squeezed my arms so tightly I could feel the bruises developing.

I tried to fight back, but that made him angrier. He leaned his forehead against mine. It was a habit of his. He'd never left bruises there, but the area would always be so tender afterward I couldn't even wear a hat for a week.

At some point, I was able to run out my back door, down my steps, through my back yard. Even though I was in bare feet, I felt nothing as I traveled over cement, dry grass, and the freshly tarred and pebbled street.

I would learn later that I had multiple cuts on my feet from the jagged edges of so many surfaces. It might have been the adrenaline, or even the shock of it all that allowed me to run without pain, I have no idea. I just know that I get it now when I hear someone talk about never feeling a thing when they're in survival mode.

Have you ever had one of those bad dreams where you can't wake up, yet no one comes to your rescue? I was living through that exact dream, well, nightmare. I ran down the street as fast as I could, yelling for help, but no one came outside.

Looking back, this seems like a plot out of a bad movie. I would be front and center on the couch yelling at the crazy woman on the screen to just DO something to save herself. But this was no movie; this was my life. And still, I couldn't believe any of this was real. This wasn't happening to me; it couldn't be happening to me. I know I didn't cry out for help any more once I realized help wasn't coming. I was on my own.

I can still remember his laugh as he caught up to me about a half block from my house.

"Do you really think your fat ass can outrun me?"

He kicked my feet out and the next thing I knew, I fell to the street. When I looked over my hands the next day, I saw where the pebbles had dug into them, but again, I hadn't felt a thing when it happened. I was so desperate to get away, but failed.

He picked me up by my hair (I had short hair then, but it hurt like hell) and dragged me back to my house. Hunched over, I struggled to keep my balance and not be pulled along the ground. I still have trouble understanding how he could overpower me. He was only five foot five—not much taller than me, but I was totally at his mercy.

At this point, the tears streamed down my face. So many tears. I was crying so hard between being scared for my life and the simple fact that he was hurting me. The entire way back, he told me how stupid I was to try to get away from him.

He wanted to see me suffer.

Once we got inside my house, he flung me into my counter. The pain shot down my lower back and into my leg. I fell to the floor. He stood over me, screaming. He told me I would never get rid of him. That I would always need to watch my back.

To this day, I hate that area of my kitchen. I can still remember sitting on the floor with him towering over me. He told me many horrible things like how I was going to die a slow death and how I would never see my children again. He knew that my two babies were my entire world. He knew this was the magic threat that would make me give in and give him my money.

I was giving in. I told him I would drive to the bank and drain my account. I convinced him I only had sixty dollars because I had just paid my mortgage. That was good enough for him.

We got into the car and drove to my bank just a few miles away. I remember the clock in my car saying 2:57 a.m. As we returned, a police officer pulled out of the gas station across from my street. My tormentor knew me well, though. He read my mind. He told me that if I did anything that I would have to watch him die at the hands of a police officer.

I turned down my street and into my driveway. He got out and walked to where his car was parked—all of this for crack.

I would like to say that I never saw him again. But that would be a lie. He convinced me yet again that he was sorry. He couldn't believe that he left the bruises that he did. He assured me he would never hurt me again.

I knew better. I had heard it before, but I still let him back into my life. I can't explain why. I wish I could. It's not like he ever bought me flowers or gifts to strengthen his message. There is no way he would spend his precious crack money on flowers or a gift, that's for sure. He was manipulative. Knew exactly what to say and how to say it.

Even though I had heard it a hundred times before, I still let him back in. Somehow, I would forget that when he was angry, his eyes would remind me of the devil.

He took a job traveling out of state for weeks at a time. Not seeing him every day helped me break free. I knew I didn't love him. I knew I was being manipulated every day. I knew that if I just didn't look him in the eyes, that I could get through this.

And I did! I bought a gun. I knew a Marine at the time and he took me out to a field and showed me how to use it with confidence. While it wasn't the first time I shot one, it was the first time I ever owned one.

I have a security system installed, but I still have nightmares. I'm always afraid that he will show up at my door. His current girlfriend put him in jail for abusing her. She had the guts to press charges. Something I couldn't get myself to do. Don't judge me. I don't know why I couldn't do it. I did and still do hate him. To this day, I wish that I had alerted that cop just so I don't have to look over my shoulders walking from my car to my house.

It's been five years since that horrible night. I have dated more losers than I can count over that time. I would finally let someone in and they would ruin my faith in humanity by saying things like, "You really should look into getting a tummy tuck" after a moment of intimacy.

Then a funny thing happened: I stopped looking at others to remind me of my own worth. I found it inside of myself.

I have this tattoo that reminds me how amazing and strong I am. It is easy for me to see because it's on the inside of my left forearm. It says: "I am enough."

I AM enough. I now have my own business, my babies are off on their own in college, and I am blessed to have built friendships with other amazing ladies. We remind each other how incredible we are, and we actually believe it.

I finally met a man. A really nice man who has his shit together and is good to me. But occasionally I ask myself: "Am I worthy?" To me, he is perfect—way too good for me. People tell me I deserve to be happy. I look happy. I am happy, but does that mean I'm worthy?

I look down at my tattoo and remind myself that yes, I certainly am.

My name is Jenny. I'm the mother of two amazing children, ages 24 and 22. I have owned a cleaning service for about 15 years and love my job! My two favorite things to do are riding my Harley and traveling.

A Recovery Story in Several Parts*

Lindsey Zelvin

Not Necessarily in Order

June 2012—Indiana

They took away my blanket; its knotted edges posed a suicide risk.

While the staff of South Shore Academy weren't aware of the irony of their action, it was not lost on me. I was given that blanket in the Pediatric ICU hours after my actual suicide attempt a month earlier. An attempt that, to be clear, did not involve a blanket.

I hadn't had it long, but the blanket had quickly become important to me. Brightly colored and comfortingly soft, a nurse placed it on my bed the morning after I was admitted. It was snuggly and warm, making the hospital slightly less scary after the chaos of the night before. I'd kept it on my bed at home ever since my release. My mom was thoughtful enough to bring it with us as she and my dad made the two-hour drive to commit me. Again.

They took my journal, too, because it was a hardback. How I was expected to harm myself or others with a magnetic journal from Barnes and Noble, I'll never know, but when dealing with "crazies" one can never be too careful.

This wasn't my first unwanted institutionalization. For the past year, I'd been in and out of partial hospitalization programs, the psych ward, and a residential treatment facility. But it wasn't the sort of thing that got easier with time. Every time I left a place like this—one where the door locked behind me like a prison cell—I promised myself I would never go back. And then I'd be locked away again. A failure and a criminal.

January 2019—Illinois

My anxiety dreams are increasing. Every time I close my eyes, I'm back in that horrible place. Afraid, lonely, and angry at everyone. I'm sick again. When I wake up, I have to remind myself none of it is real. I am healthy(ish). But more importantly, I'm no longer a monster capable of causing that kind of damage.

I've been trying to write the story of my last hospitalization. The place that "saved me." Except, it didn't. Save me, I mean. It arrested my fall, stopped me from spiraling into oblivion, but the months after were miserable. Quite possibly the loneliest of my life. They made me long for the safety of an institution. In those places, I may have been locked away but at least I wasn't isolated. Everyone there was like me: struggling with themselves, the real world too much for all of us. But when I returned to high school, I found myself behind academically, socially, and emotionally. My friends were busy being normal teenagers while I still had to figure out what normal meant. Everything I'd ever feared had come to pass. I was completely alone.

So this attempted documentation brings back a lot of pain and disappointment. Because after the "revelations" that occurred at that place I thought I would finally be better. Happy and healthy for the first time in two years. Instead, I found myself more lost than ever.

But does that matter? Does what happened "after" negate the tremendous growth that occurred during? Growth that gave me the strength to keep going even when it seemed like everything was falling apart, the strength that I would eventually use to rebuild my life. I don't know. But the fact that I'm still thinking about it, still writing about it, over six years later seems to suggest there's a story here I need to tell.

July 2011-August 2012—Illinois, Wisconsin, Indiana

I read a lot of books while I was in treatment. There's not much else to do when you're locked away from the world "for your own safety." At least that's the reason my parents gave. I believed them in a way. I knew they loved me, I couldn't have destroyed them the way I did if they didn't, but I'd been doing this long enough to know that treatment is the place parents send their kids when they've run out of ideas. A "good girl's" version of rehab.

I was severely anorexic. Hence the frequent hospitalizations. I didn't want food anywhere near me; I panicked any time it came close. At my worst, I washed my hands so much they cracked and bled because I was afraid of transmitting calories through touch. Starving myself was something in which I took a sick kind of pride. I didn't need food; I did better without it, even if my parents and doctors didn't see it that way. Hence the treatment centers, places designed to refeed and rehabilitate the malnourished in the hope of one day introducing us back into society.

But a person can only starve themselves for so long before something gives way. Eventually, food was forced back into my life. And it was agonizing. Like pouring cement down my throat and feeling it harden in my belly over and over again. Somehow I was expected to claw my way back to normalcy. To make peace with the pit in my stomach and go about my daily life as best I could.

Except... I couldn't.

January 2012—Wisconsin

It was the first time I'd been away from my parents for longer than a few days. They didn't tell me I was going until I was already in the car. I sobbed the whole way there—heavy, ugly sobs that sounded more like they came from a wounded animal than a teenage girl.

I'm pretty sure I considered jumping out and making a run for it because I remember the sound of my father child-locking the doors. It's a bit humiliating, being treated like a toddler at fifteen, but that's what you get when you start throwing temper tantrums, running away from doctor's appointments, and threatening to kill yourself.

I can't pretend I don't understand why they did it. But in that moment, walking into the Eating Disorder Center (EDC) at Rogers Memorial Hospital, two hours away from home—not knowing if I was freezing from the building's poor heating system, the winter weather, or lack of body fat—it felt like life as I knew it was over. How could anything ever be the same after my parents left me in a place like this?

They were giving up on me.

All I wanted to do was snuggle close to my mom and never let go. I wanted to convince her to get back in the car, take me home, and pretend this never happened. I would promise to be better like I had so many times before. But there are only so many empty promises a mother can accept, especially when she's watching her daughter devolve into a demon before her eyes. I knew my parents would leave this place without me. But I didn't know when they were coming back, or whether they even wanted to.

I wrapped my arms around myself to ward off the chill.

January 2019—Illinois

My body still struggles to regulate temperature.

I don't know if this is a relatively new phenomenon, connected to my irksome habit of starving myself since puberty, or something I've dealt with all my life. To be honest, memories of my body before the eating disorder are fuzzy at best. When you've been hyperaware of every calorie you've consumed since the age of thirteen, more body-positive memories tend to fade into the background. Now nearly every sense memory I have connects in one way or another to how I have abused myself over the years.

I can't even blame my body; it's only reacting to what it knows.

It's not my body's fault that every winter, as the temperature drops and the darkness comes, I find myself increasingly afraid to venture outside. Because the way the wind tightens around me and the feeling of the chill seeping into my bones reminds me of how difficult it is to get warm when you've stolen all the fat from your body. Because even walking across campus reminds me…

December 2011—Illinois

…of when I walked four miles in the snow, in the dark, after a fight with my mom to escape…what? Her? My illness? My life? Me? All I know is I couldn't stop walking. I remember wearing high heeled boots and a skirt that left my legs exposed to the cold, both fearing and reveling in the numbness climbing up my body.

I did a lot of walking at night when I was at my sickest. I think it was because there were fewer people around, less chance of running into someone and having to pretend to be a real person. It's easier to hide in the dark.

I feel most vulnerable in the winter.

June 2012—Indiana

South Shore Academy was very different from the EDC. Instead of Oconomowoc, Wisconsin—a picturesque campus which included many different program houses, a ropes course, a gym, and expansive grounds with gorgeous paths, blanketed in fluffy white snow—I found myself entering a small building in an industrial park in Valparaiso, Indiana, surrounded by fast food places, a methadone clinic on the first floor, and a YMCA a little down the way.

Rogers had appeared a sanctuary for rest and reflection while its residents learned to love themselves again. South Shore looked like the facility to which parents sent their troubled teens when they ran out of options. The end of the line.

The first thing I noticed was the air conditioning, or lack thereof. June in Valparaiso was hot, upwards of ninety degrees Fahrenheit for most of the summer. Sweat was a permanent state of being. The staff explained (to my parents of course, not me) that they'd been having trouble with the system, but it should be fixed within the next few days. It took a week.

By the end of my stay, the air conditioning had broken at least four more times. We often found ourselves sleeping in the gym to fight the heat.

Every summer since 2012—Illinois

When I'm too hot, I feel exhausted, gluttonous, and large. The sun exposes my lack of substance and I find myself wanting to evaporate to escape judgment. Summer turns me into a large, hulking presence wanting nothing more than to disappear.

When it starts to get warmer outside, it feels like life is returning to the world. Everything becomes green and bright and colorful again. But then the sun just keeps getting brighter and the temperature starts to rise. Everyone wears shorts and crop tops, bathing suits and sundresses. Bodies are on display for the entire world to see, glorying in the sunlight and the promise it brings. But I am too much:

Too short,

Too chubby,

Too sweaty,

Too pale,

Too blotchy,

Too ugly,

Too unreal, to be seen in such brightness, exposed in such a way. To be made real by the sunlight.

January 2019—Illinois

I didn't have any dreams last night. Maybe it's because I finally managed to commit some of these experiences to paper. To make them real, rather than the stuff of nightmares. I mean, they were real once upon a time, but it's been so long now that it feels like another life.

In my day-to-day, I try not to dwell on my worst experiences. I tell the funny stories about the bad food in the psych ward and the time I tried vegan chili while they were re-feeding me, fueling my disgust for beans and chickpeas for the rest of my life.

I talk about the girls in my program at Rogers who used to flirt with the boys who lived in the basement (because what better place to find love than an eating disorder treatment center?) and obsessed over when we'd have programming with them again.

I talk about my horror movie phase halfway through my first stay in residential after seeing *The Woman in Black* on one of our weekly outings, and the big white van that made us look insanely suspicious whenever we went anywhere.

These are the stories that make people laugh. The quirky tidbits that remind the outside world we are still human. The anecdotes that make their way into big budget movies. The moments of levity that help the characters (and the audience) forget where they are. These are the stories I'm allowed to tell in public, despite the very likely chance someone will look down on me for making light of something as serious as a hospitalization for mental illness. There's an even better chance that any person espousing this sort of view has never been hospitalized for mental illness in their life and has no clue what they're talking about.

These are the acceptable stories. Because no one wants to hear the dark ones. That's what the movies are for: experiencing trauma vicariously through other people. If I start talking about it freely, then I bring the danger out into the open. My crazy forces other people to think about their crazy, or the crazy of those they love, and that's just too close to home.

So I write about it instead. It's much more acceptable in polite society. I use my trauma as material and I turn it into something worthwhile. Or I try to, at least.

A couple years ago, I wrote a journal entry connecting writing to bloodletting. I described it as a release of toxicity, not necessarily in the substance that comes out on the page, but in how the process of putting pen to paper (or in this case, fingers to keys) burns away the chemical that runs through my veins and makes me miserable. Kind of like cooking with alcohol I guess (not that I'd know, since I can't cook to save my life). The point is I'm left with a product that, in its essence, is good. Flawed, possibly overdone, but good. I'm just hoping I'm a better writer than I am a cook.

February 2012—Wisconsin

I was a bit overeager the first time I tried to write my "recovery story," considering I hadn't recovered yet and was nowhere near close.

I'd been in residential treatment for less than two weeks. Relieved to have moved out of the hospital ward-like setting of inpatient, I was determined to make this stay my last. I received an assignment from my therapist to chronicle "my disorder" and I took it to heart, filling ten pages of the magnetic hardback journal that would be taken away from me a few months later at South Shore Academy.

This was the first time I thought about trying to write down everything that had happened over the past two years and turn it into something. The genesis of the idea that if I could make sense of what had happened to me—why and how I got sick—then I could overcome it and move on. And then, maybe all this suffering would have a purpose.

It was an idea I'd return to over and over again during the next six and a half years.

June 2012—Indiana

South Shore was kind of insane. Not only was I not allowed my journal, I wasn't even allowed a pencil for the first week. Even after this trial period, pencils were only allowed for use in the classroom (although I eventually managed to convince the teacher to allow me one while doing schoolwork outside the prescribed time and place). This meant that if I wanted to journal or work on anything non-school related, I had to use a marker. I found it a bit too infantilizing to use markers on a regular basis.

The teacher hated me. Peggy had a curriculum, and she wanted all her students to follow it. But I, rebel that I am, came prepared with my own. This made her unhappy. When I tried to politely explain to her that I was finishing my sophomore year of high school remotely, she insisted I do as she directed, which involved reading and writing a one-page summary of George Orwell's *Animal Farm*.

Please forgive me when I say, in the least arrogant way possible, her curriculum was not nearly as difficult as mine; I would've been bored out of my mind. More importantly, though, I desperately needed to finish my classes by the end of the summer if I wanted to be able to start junior year in the fall with the rest of my classmates. Falling behind was not an option. But Peggy took my insistence and anxiety for disobedience, endeavoring to punish and shame in order to force me in line with the rest of the inmates.

I refused to be bullied. I'd had enough of that at Rogers from the girls I was supposed to "recover" with and from the "teachers" in the psych ward who would yell at me every time I fell asleep during "school," despite their knowledge that one of the side effects of my new medication was drowsiness. I was incarcerated, not incompetent. I was intelligent and determinedly stubborn enough not to let an insecure teacher with a power complex get in the way of my scholastic achievements.

I called my parents that night. They called her the next morning. She never actually apologized to me, but she left me alone to do my work after that.

Take that, Peggy.

March 2010—Illinois

I was always smart. A smart ass sometimes but smart, nonetheless. My mom used to tell me I was nine going on forty and this remained a point of pride for many years to follow. I was never the prettiest, or the most popular, but I was bright and I worked hard. These were my defining characteristics during my formative years.

I was also anxious. And the combination of intelligence and anxiety led to a condition I could never shake: Perfectionism. Everything I did had to be perfect, otherwise what was the point? If I couldn't be the best—the smartest—I was nothing. Because what else did I have to offer?

My parents always emphasized the importance of being a good person. They never put pressure on me to be the best at anything except being myself. All they wanted was for me to be kind and try my best. But even that managed to become warped. Instead of just treating others how I wanted to be treated, I obsessed over every little thing. Afraid of thinking something mean or accidentally saying the wrong thing, I would replay conversations and actions in my head over and over, worrying that I'd somehow hurt or offended somebody.

If I wasn't a good enough person, a smart enough person, a worthy enough person, I wasn't enough. And if I wasn't enough then what business did I have taking up space?

I guess that's why I began to shrink myself.

June-August 2012—Indiana

I despised Rebecca, the therapist at South Shore Academy, on sight. I was sick of therapists, of people who thought they understood what I needed—who thought they understood me—without even trying to see what I was going through. I was sick of arrogant people who preached from a position of power and privilege without the experience to back it up. I'd had enough.

In our first session, I walked out. It was a signature move of mine. I was an old pro at the dramatic exit. I told her I never wanted to see her again.

She simply looked at me. Then she said, "Okay. Come back when you're ready."

I came back the next week.

I'm not sure exactly how or why I started to trust her. Maybe it was because she hadn't chased after me and forced me back into the session. Maybe it was that she seemed to understand I needed someone who respected my need for autonomy but refused to be my emotional punching bag. Or maybe I was just ready to stop being so angry.

It turned out that Rebecca had had anorexia too. From age thirteen to twenty-three, she'd struggled, suffering a heart attack in the process. She told me that she went for a run and felt a massive pain in her chest that brought her to her knees. Then she got up and finished the run. She only found out later that it was a heart attack. This may sound crazy to "normal" people. But it just made my heart hurt. I knew exactly how she felt.

Her parents had also shipped her from treatment center to treatment center until she finally found her way to recovery. And I knew she was really in recovery because she always kept cookies and chocolate in her desk. She'd offer them to me sometimes, but I struggled to take them.

To be embarrassingly, regretfully honest, I was scared. Rebecca wasn't overweight, but she wasn't thin. Not even close. If I got into recovery, would I look like that? Would I be bigger than I was when I started this whole thing? I felt terrible for judging her but I couldn't help it. The thought kept getting stuck in my head.

I think she knew. I never said anything, but she was too smart not to know. When I asked her how she'd stayed in recovery so long, she told me she'd reached a place where she was happy with her life. She could play with her little niece and nephew without getting winded. She could go out to dinner with her friends without worrying about what to order. She could live her life the way she wanted. And her body made that possible.

Rebecca described recovery to me as backing away from a cliff. "It's always there," she said, "the cliff never fades from view but somehow you work your way back from the edge. And eventually you get far enough away that you're no longer in danger of falling off. That," she told me, "is recovery."

For the first time, it made sense. And for the first time, I believed it was possible.

April 2017—Oxford

I was never bulimic. It's something I made a point of saying at all the treatment centers. I was anorexic. Period.

But at this point, I was neither. I was a stressed-out Oxford student in need of release so I could finish my work. At least that's what I told myself as I knelt down in front of the toilet and pushed my fingers down my throat.

I felt my knees groan in protest against the unforgiving tile and I was grateful for the pain. It was comforting; it grounded me. My eyes began to water and my nose started to drip as I shoved my fingers further down my throat until I felt the first wave build up inside me.

I emptied myself into the toilet bowl until there was nothing left. Then I forced my hand back down, shoving my fingers against my tonsils until it felt like my throat might bleed. Again and again the hand went back down. I looked into the bowl.

It still didn't feel like enough, but I felt a bit better. Maybe now I could finish my paper.

January 2019—Illinois

Purging was never a part of my eating disorder. It was dirty and messy and far more ineffective than straight starvation. Plus, until April of 2017, I didn't even think it was possible. I've learned since that it's much easier to resist something you think you cannot do.

I still don't consider myself bulimic. I've purged maybe eight times in my life (even if those times did all occur in the past two years). Recovery or not, food is still hard for me. And purging felt like a one-time thing: a last resort rather than a way of life. An undo button for when I've been gluttonous, gross, and weak. After I finish there's a sense of relief and unburdening, even if it's immediately followed by the knowledge of the inadequacy of my offering. In those moments, if I had to stick my fingers down my throat until my tonsils were red and raw, it was worth it. For a moment, I was free. There was no cement in my belly.

I know that it's not a one-time thing. An addict is still an addict, and trading one disorder for another doesn't change that. I fight it, the way I have many other temptations over the years, and when it does happen, I make sure to reach out to a person I trust to help me process. They remind me that a slip is not a relapse, that it doesn't make me a bad person, and that it doesn't undo all the work I've done to get to where I am.

I am a work in progress. The quality of said work may be questionable at times, but I keep at it as best I can. It's the only way I know how to survive. And considering the fact of my survival was still in question half a decade ago, I think I can take the liberty of marking my continued existence in the victory column.

―――~

Lindsey is a writer and practice-based PhD student in Narrative Nonfiction at the University of Kent in Canterbury where she is currently crafting her hybrid memoir. She received her Bachelor of Arts in English magna cum laude from the College of Wooster before traveling across the pond for her Master of Arts in Creative Writing with English Literary Studies at Lancaster University. She is a prose writer whose research examines representations of mental illness in literature. Her PhD draws on narratology, medical humanities, the genre of memoir, and trauma theory to create more authentic and ethical representations of chronic mental illness within her writing.

LAYERS OF ME

Edna J. White

I was only five years old when it began—just a child. I was an expressive, busy yet serious, little girl who loved to laugh and sing around the house.

To him, I was just somebody of his sickest circumstance. He always had his eyes on me, and "the incidents," as I refer to them now, became routine. So routine that I thought it was normal.

He touched me every opportunity he had. He didn't care about the time of day or who was home. All he needed was a five-minute window, and he took advantage.

I always felt so dirty afterwards that I would shower with a Brillo pad till my skin was red and painful. I knew what he was doing was wrong, but he always looked me in my eyes and told me never to tell. I kept his secret even when I wanted to tell; the gifts that I received duped me into silence.

Then one day, a few months before my ninth birthday, I finally told. He didn't deny it, yet begged for forgiveness. My family believed me all the while separating us, but we never spoke about it again.

We continued on with Sunday dinners and big family functions as if nothing ever happened. It was like they locked it up in the box of "things that never happened." And I, like everyone else, threw away the key and believed that lie.

In my mid-twenties, I struggled in relationships from those painful memories. I never brought it up because I know he's loved—a father, a husband, an uncle, a grandfather. The idea of tainting his reputation was just too much for me to bear. So, I've been carrying that burden for a long time—until now.

I don't proclaim to be a doctor or a psychologist, yet a continuous survivor of the illness of another that has ravaged my life and adversely affected me.

Yes, I took critical steps with counselors, God, and finally within myself to heal. At a crossroads in my life now, I still have unanswered questions and I frantically want to understand how my childhood sexual abuse has affected my adulthood. What happened in that house for all those years was a violation of my innocent mind, body, and spirit.

How do I move on?

How do I erase the painful memories that constantly come back to haunt me? Things that I thought I never knew, suppressed so far back in my memory and are easily triggered by smells, TV theme songs from the 90s, and even patterns on fabric.

In the sessions with my psychologist, I was able to bring out the stuffed-down pain that was disguised as silence. For years, I put off writing about how I felt because of the "shame" of shaming my mother, my aunt, my sisters, my children and family, yet I woke up this morning and realized at age forty-nine that it's a subtle secret of silence.

For a person who has been sexually abused, I always heard "What happens in our house, stays in our house" and "We don't talk about these things."

But I don't want my children to inherit the lies that I have internalized, and I don't want to not share information with them. I believe that most families don't talk about sex, let alone sexual abuse.

Many survivors bury sexual abuse so deeply inside that we would never connect it to today's physical illness and pain, depression or addiction, inability to hold a job or get out of debt, dissatisfaction in a relationship, inability to nurture our children, or why we can't simply say no to people or situations that do us harm.

It took me to this age to master some of these things, and I still struggle with the realization that my past sexual abuse urgently impacts my life now. I had begun to peel away things that I thought were everyday life responses. However, that wasn't the case. The self-awareness bug would slap me in the face, yet again.

Through this six-year journey I had no self-confidence even though I displayed the proverbial poker face. We don't tell enough stories about abuse or how to survive it.

Yes, we hear the blame but we don't hear about what it takes to come back after this has taken over our lives, invaded our egos, and partaken of our bodies. The damage done to us would invade our eating habits, our responses to perceived dynamics, and failures to our bodies.

Each of us crying out, yet not to be heard in silence. We endure every day reliving the initial shock of the misguided responses from our trusted deliverers to our first "out," over and over like "Groundhog Day."

Again and again we live in isolation.

We never stop thinking about what happened, and we are always giving out "should have" and "could have" shame. Alone with shame and its dreadful reactions to choices, to kill the pain.

I want to share with you some main points that I learned, and I wish that someone had told me what emotions and fears I would experience.

I worried that people would not believe me when I did report it, or worse, I would be punished for sharing the family secret.

This is a difficult topic to write about and a hard topic to read about as well. The thought of anyone using a child to gratify his own perverse sexual desires is an incomprehensible evil. It is an evil that has disgraced, destroyed, and devalued the human race.

But it's real.

It happens and the numbers of those affected by it are growing. Maybe it has happened to you.

I understand that you may want to stop reading at this point. If you have memories of sexual abuse, it can be painful to revisit those memories and the emotions associated with them. Or maybe you are someone who has no memory of abuse, but you have a feeling that you were abused. You occasionally get an image of an event, a person, or of yourself in an uncomfortable situation, and you wonder.

Perhaps there is someone in your past that causes negative emotions to surface whenever you think of them or have to be around them. Again you wonder but don't know for sure. Maybe you don't want to know.

If so, I understand. What you're feeling is typical. You've survived by shoving the abuse, the memories, that "wondering feeling" deep down so that you could get on with your life.

Or you have minimized the abuse you do remember by saying, "It really was not that big of a deal." But lately it has been surfacing unexpectedly. You're no longer able to keep it buried. It's having an impact on your dreams, your marriage, your parenting, your ability to trust, and to be intimate. Perhaps you need answers to questions like, "Am I this way because of what happened to me as a child?"

But there may be another reason you'd rather not keep reading. Shame. The shame that whispers, "You're to blame. You didn't say no. You asked for it. You wanted it. You allowed it to continue. It's. All. Your. Fault!" I've led hundreds of women through sexual healing, and more than half of them experienced some form of sexual abuse or trauma, as in rape. And every single one of them had, at some point, believed that they were to blame.

It's a lie, a horrible, evil lie! You were not to blame. It was not your fault. You were a child. Children have no sexual desire, unless that sexual desire is awakened against their will. I'm praying for you. Praying that you won't let the shame, fear, or the lies keep you from claiming the truth. Truth is this: You are not alone. It wasn't your fault. You can be healed. There is hope.

My connection between sexual abuse and developing an eating disorder entangled the guilt, shame, anesthesia, self-punishment, soothing, comfort, protection, and rage. I was given some foods in my younger years to calm me in order for the abuse to continue.

I now know that the very things that I was bribed with became ingrained into my psyche.

Crackers, cheese, chocolate, and the right not to eat what my siblings had to eat. As I got older, I ate very little and actually kept food in my room so that I had control of what I ate.

Sexual abuse can have many effects on the eating habits and body image of survivors. Sexual abuse violates the boundaries of the self so dramatically that inner sensations of hunger, fatigue, or sexuality become difficult to identify.

We who have been sexually abused may turn to food to relieve a wide range of different states of tension that have nothing to do with hunger. It is that confusion and uncertainty about my inner perceptions that lead me to focus on the food, whether little or a lot.

It is said that many survivors of sexual abuse often work to become very fat or very thin in an attempt to render themselves unattractive. In this way, they try to de-sexualize themselves. I became a tomboy!

Other survivors obsessively diet, starve, or purge to make their bodies "perfect." a perfect body is a survivor's attempt to feel more powerful, invulnerable, and in control, so as not to re-experience the powerlessness felt as a child.

In the reverse, some large men and women who are survivors of sexual abuse are afraid to lose weight because it will render them feeling smaller and childlike. Padding themselves like protection.

I can hear some of you saying to yourself, "But I've done all the counseling. I've tried everything I can think of, and nothing has worked." You may not like my answer, but I'm going to encourage you to not give up.

Don't give up.

Healing is a journey, a process. It doesn't happen overnight.

Many survivors experience frequent crises like job disappointments or relocations, failed relationships, or financial setbacks.

Many of these crises are the result of unresolved childhood abuse issues.

The reasons are complex, but the ongoing internal chaos in many survivors prevents the establishment of regularity, predictability, and consistency.

Many survivors function in "crisis mode," responding with stopgap measures that don't resolve the underlying issues like denial, a form of forgetting (putting it out of our minds), and sometimes sex or drugs.

This can be exhausting and dispiriting and contribute to feelings of helplessness and hopelessness.

Someone touching me made me cringe and sometimes made me nauseous. Sometimes I would projectile vomit during intimacy. I hated facial hair on men for many years. All the responses from the theft of my innocence because of him.

Dark cellars or basements were totally off limits for me in my adult life. I never knew why until I used the tools of meditation to clear my many thoughts, which I called daydreaming. I was escaping in my mind to a place I understood, because it was the one place I could control.

My mind kept busy to not notice or hear what I needed to face.

No matter how much time had passed, unresolved childhood traumas wreaked havoc on my personal life and the lives of the people around me.

This was especially true when it came to romantic relationships because these, in particular, required a great deal of trust and intimacy.

Victims of childhood abuse are not always comfortable with others close to them; early experiences taught them that loved ones were not to be trusted and that safety and security were merely fairy tales.

Decades later, even when in a loving and supportive relationship, some survivors still cannot erase those false scripts from their heads and wholly embrace a loving partner.

Lack of trust can manifest in different ways. Some people become haunted by insecurity and doubt, which leads them to become jealous and suspicious of a partner even when there is no reason to suspect infidelity. They might need to be constantly reassured of a partner's love.

Other people might push their loved ones away, refusing to make deep and lasting connections for fear of getting hurt again. They would rather live a life of isolation and loneliness than become vulnerable and intimate with another person.

I was stuck in a cycle of abuse. People thought for me, talked for me, demeaned me, and did what they wanted to me. This is known as repetition compulsion, and it describes the pattern where victims of trauma find themselves constantly reliving the abuse.

I was a young girl who was physically abused by a father figure and found herself constantly seeking out abusive and unavailable men. Although I did not realize it at the time, I was choosing these bad boyfriends because I subconsciously wanted to recreate the trauma and "fix" the situation.

I tried to be "good enough" for my partners, to be sweet enough, pretty enough, smart enough, obedient enough to earn my partner's love and hence rewrite history. If I could accept someone who really paid attention to me, then I would finally get that unconditional, supportive love I was never offered. I would be fulfilled.

I failed miserably.

Of course, the chances of that result are slim because any partner who resembles my stepfather (angry, violent, aggressive, withholding, and so forth) will not ever be likely to offer me love and respect.

Hence, I was caught up in a cycle of unhealthy relationships, constantly choosing partners who were disrespectful and violent and unavailable.

Addressing the wounds of childhood takes therapy.

I can remember that the day of reckoning for me was while walking from my friend's house after a night of drinking. As I walked closer to my house, I began to see what my life really was—a prison.

I cried.

I was seventeen years old carrying my eight-month-old son, sobbing uncontrollably because the abuse was still fresh and never dealt with.

The next thing I remember was that I was sitting on the railroad track in the dark, my son playing and smiling and wiping my tears.

The train never came.

I walked home and I remember thinking I can't even commit suicide right. But there was a bigger destiny that I didn't even know.

I cried for two days straight and no one except my brother realized it.

Help came as I rode the bus that next day with my son, tears streaming from my eyes and my jubilant son wiping my face. A lady walked past me, touched my shoulder and whispered, "You may need this." It was a business card of a local therapist.

I didn't know it then, but my journey to healing would soon begin.

A therapist who specializes in childhood abuse will be able to offer the assistance and resources needed to finally break the chain of abuse. Everyone deserves a life that is filled with love, respect, and hope, and such a world can exist only if the wounded child that is still suffering inside gets treated.

It would be years later that I began therapy again, as life took on that same circle, because my little girl was still in pain.

Healing is a decision I continue to make every day. It is the day that you recognize the effects of trauma in your life, and you need to make an active commitment to heal.

Deep healing happens only when you choose it and if you're willing to change, and that is a daily commitment. I continue to use the tools my therapist taught me, and I work on myself every day.

Healing is tough, yet when you commit to it, you show that you actually care about yourself.

Yeah, I had to give myself a voice. I lost it a long time ago and the only way my little girl wouldn't have the pain anymore was if she spoke out.

I had to deal with the memories and the pain. I had to deal with the disbelief of what I really went through with my family.

Listen, it doesn't get better until it gets worse and I learned that the hard way. But I also learned that way.

There is going to be shame with this healing journey no matter what. You're going to doubt what you remember. You're going to doubt if anybody believes you. You're going to doubt yourself, but you must always speak out, speak it out, get it out of you.

This story is called "Layers of Me" because I think of myself as an onion. The analogy came from a time when I was cooking with my mother and she would ask me to peel the onions.

I had tried all the remedies, yet the onion peeling still irritated my eyes. One day, she handed me some tiny onions and asked me to put them on the tray. I wondered why I didn't have to peel them.

"Mom, do you want me to peel those?"

She looked at me and said, "No. Those are sweet."

I frowned and spoke with some agitation. "Then why wouldn't you let me peel those? I wouldn't have cried so much!"

She leaned down and softly laughed. "Those are the sweet part of the big onions once they are grown."

That story stayed with me and gave me a life lesson.

It takes a very long time to get down to the sweetest part, and along the way there will be tears because you're peeling layers back. Those layers will reveal so much about you, about why you do it, about what you feel.

The onion can be multiple colors and sizes, but one thing is for certain: All of them have a sweet spot. There is a sweet spot in me, and because I kept looking, searching, feeling, and using my voice, I was able to break my silence.

I didn't want to be in my own way anymore. I wanted to be happy, and if it took years to heal, years to learn about myself, and years to uncover myself, I was going to do it.

Any of us who have gone through it can do it.

Edna J. White is an author, teacher, life coach, and motivational speaker who helps essential professionals unlock their full potential. The majority of her clients that are involved in extremely high-stress environments include CEOs, start-up founders, entrepreneurs, and those transitioning in their careers.

She founded 2nd Chance Services to help transform the mindsets from "I'm lost" to "I'm in control of my life." Her movement is centered on the belief that cultural conditioning must be broken in order for women to live a life with confidence, freedom, and happiness.

The programs that Edna and her team designed are based on real-life experiences, encompassing eight key areas in life: finances, physical health, mental and emotional health, lifestyle, love and relationships, career, family and friends, and spiritual growth.

Edna's unique coaching system leverages mindset training and high-performance strategies that help eliminate fears and break down any mental roadblocks that get in the way.

THE WOW FACTOR

Lakisha Wilson

Have you ever been through recurring tragic events? Where you endure pain and loss over and over again until you think your pain and loss will never end? I recently experienced a string of tragedies where I lost loved ones over such a short span of time I had no chance to grieve or mourn before I was hit with yet another loss. It seemed never-ending, and there was a period of time I wondered how I could ever recover from it all.

First, we lost the guardian of the house, the family dog, Storm. He was a beautiful husky. No one dared to enter our home without approval from Storm.

Three months after Storm passed, we lost my grandfather, the breadwinner and foundation of the home, to the robbing illness known as Alzheimer's.

Three months later, we lost my baby brother at the young age of fifteen by the hands of someone he once called "friend." One hit after another.

While trying to deal with the trauma we already had been faced with, we lost my best friend, my go-to, my spiritual advisor—my grandmother. She had been secretly battling cancer.

My grandmother had been the backbone of our family. Everyone thought the worst would come of me after losing her, but it was because of her teaching through love, guidance, and determination that all I can do is smile and be grateful to have been blessed with such an Angel in my life.

I look back at how far we have come as a family unit. It was very shaky at first. We blamed one another and we also distanced ourselves from each other. Suddenly, out of nowhere, the *wow factor* hit me—this wasn't how we were raised or taught!

I realized we were acting out of hurt. We didn't know how to cope with so much pain and loss. So much had been laid upon us. We never had a chance to heal or mourn after one loss before we were hit with another. We were overwhelmed and burdened with so much. This was the great *wow factor*.

I put a dinner together to start the healing process. It turned out to be the best move I ever made. We had lost a lot that was precious to us, but it had taken what was most valuable to help us begin the healing process.

Family is all we have. Family is my *wow factor*. Family may take you on a roller coaster ride of emotions, but it's the strongest thing that we have. Family is guaranteed to us because they are ours and we are theirs. No matter what: when you're in need, do for those what you desire to be done for you. After that, the rest isn't our business. Once learned and received, the *wow factor* has been activated.

Spiritual woman, daughter, mother, wife, sister, and friend—wearing many hats and carrying many titles—I am a walking book of defeating and overcoming trials and tribulations while still being able to smile.

"Understanding and accepting change in life gives you the strength to get up and wear the scars gracefully."— L.M.W.

DUAL DIAGNOSIS

T Nicole Cirone

At the time of my husband's breakdown, I am 80 miles away at my parents' shore house in Ocean City, New Jersey, trying to wrap my head around my failing marriage. It is just a few weeks shy of our third wedding anniversary.

Things between my husband and me have been deteriorating for months, as his drinking and partying have become problematic and his time at home increasingly rare. By the time the 4th of July came around, we were barely speaking and hadn't shared a smile in weeks.

We had family from Texas in town for the holiday. My husband and I, playing the good host and hostess, took them to our favorite night spots. We danced and drank mojitos at Cuba Libre, and then bar-hopped around Old City well into the night. My husband and I laughed and danced together for the first time in a long time; for a moment, it seemed like old times again—when a night out was fun and didn't end in an alcohol-induced argument or with one of us behind a locked door and the other sleeping on the couch.

Though we didn't make love or even kiss that night, we slept in the same bed. That felt like a small step toward something like reconnection. But the next day, when my mother *strongly suggested* in our morning phone call, which my husband overheard from the next room, that my husband shouldn't come to the shore for the July 4th festivities "because no one wants to hear the two of you fight all week," all of the tension my husband and I had been holding in for weeks exploded.

He roared, "I don't know if I love you anymore, Nicole. This marriage was a mistake," before disappearing into our bedroom and locking the door.

"Fine, I'm out of here. Good bye!" I screamed at the other side of the door. I took the cat and drove to the shore.

I was glad to be away from him. "The salt air cures all that ails you," my grandmother used to say. As a child, I used to take long walks on the beach with her, and it seemed like everything was right as we collected shells and watched the sun rise in a diamond-like shimmer over the waves. Those memories stayed with me as I grew up, and each time I faced uncertainty or difficulty in life, I returned to find refuge in the calming presence of the beach and the ceaseless rhythm of the ocean. I settled into my shorehouse bed with my cat curled up at my feet and looked forward to the time with my family and our epic Pictionary games.

Maybe I just needed a break from my husband and his cycle of drinking binges, followed by his hangover-induced moodiness. My own anger was approaching the boiling point, after waiting up most nights for him to come home; he missed train after train. While he was sleeping it off in a blanket cocoon for a few days, I cooked, cleaned, ran the household, worked all day, took my daughter to her activities and generally made sure all of the grown-up respon-sibilities were handled. I started to feel like I had an irresponsible college student houseguest living with me, instead of a husband who was supposed to be a partner in this adulthood stuff.

We couldn't go on like this, I knew, but I was so caught up in the day-to-day with him, I no longer even knew who I was without him. For better or for worse. The "better" meant shared jokes, fun nights out in the city, evening walks, family barbecues, pizza and movie nights, that one time we filled the backyard with a giant slip-n-slide for my daughter and nephew. The "worse" meant waiting up for him as he drunk-texted me from a bar in New York, where he worked; or called me, after no contact for a whole day, from Penn Station, not knowing how he got there.

Most of all, I couldn't see beyond the rollercoaster that ranged from "You're a whore, a real piece of shit, Nicole" when he was drunk to "I'm sorry—I love you and didn't mean to say that," followed by promises to be a "better man" when he was sober. I was in survival mode all the time and was in too much shock to even realize it.

I had to start preparing myself emotionally for the divorce that seemed imminent—we'd thrown divorce around pretty much every time we'd fought, increasingly so lately, but this time it seemed he meant it. And maybe I did, too. I was seriously sick of his shit. I should have known a year into this, with all the fighting and all the drama, that this wasn't a good marriage. Yet, here we were, almost exactly three years into it, still together, with the bad days starting to outweigh the good. And other people were starting to see the ugly truth of the situation.

———

The salt air normally has a soporific effect on me, yet tonight I am wide awake and anxiety-ridden in the too-quiet house. Starting at around midnight, I receive a flurry of texts from him, the first of which read: *I'm moving out. Don't come home until I am gone. I don't EVER want to see you again.*

Fine, good, I think, that makes it easy. *Let me know when you're gone*, I text back.

Later in the night, after closing time at the local bar, text alerts from him punctuate my inbox. I know from the tone and the misspellings that he has been drinking heavily.

my computer password is XXXX; then, a few minutes later, *its time to say goodbye, nicole.*

What the hell do you mean? I text back. *So, we are really getting a divorce?*

No response. Asshole. In full-on fight mode, I keep my phone next to me on the pillow. I am angry and ready to let him have it. "Whatever you do, don't back my daughter into a corner," my dad had warned my husband before he married me. "If you do, she will strike. Like a viper." I wait, half-awake but emotionally ready to strike back at whatever nastygram pierces my inbox. Like a viper in the grass.

At 3:30 in the morning, this text chimes me awake: *tried to kill myself but im ok now.*

What the fuck. I text and call him over and over—no response. The call goes right to voicemail each time. Now in a panic, I call a suicide hotline at a crisis center. My husband had threatened suicide twice during the course of our marriage. There was no action taken either time, "just" threats—but my therapist feared his next step would be acting on his words and had recently given me a plan with the right steps to take and the order in which to take them.

The hotline at the crisis center advises me that calling 911 is the best solution in this situation, with me being 80 miles away. On the phone to 911, I explain that I am calling from the shore, that I need help, that he needs help, that someone has to go out to the house right away because my husband has threatened suicide. The responder promises to send police right away. I start to pack my bags to drive home.

But as I am leaving, my husband texts me, and he is colossally pissed off. When the police went out to our house, he sent them away, telling them we'd had a fight and I was being vindictive. He must have been stable enough by the time they arrived to convince them that his crazy wife was just trying to make him look bad, but then, my husband was one of those extra charming people who could sell hellfire to the devil himself—even when he was out of his mind.

Ill check myself into the hospital tomorrow, he texts, *but I don't want to see you.*

—

My parents weigh in on the situation a few hours later over morning coffee at the kitchen table. They live next door to us at home in Philly. The best part about that is that they are there to babysit my daughter. We have weekly Sunday family dinners. And we can just run back and forth between the driveway or call to each other from kitchen window to kitchen window. Just like in the old world.

The downside to living next door to my parents is that they hear some of our more epic fights; they know that we are having major issues yet again, which was why he wasn't welcome at the shore, and they convince me at the breakfast table that I should stay at the shore and just let him move out, like he said he was going to. "Nicole, please listen to us. You're making a fool of yourself. It's time to break the cycle. Let him go."

I take my third cup of coffee out on the porch, in an attempt to collect my thoughts. My parents are right. But I still love my husband. And on a deeper level, one I cannot bring myself to discuss with them, I am gravely afraid to be alone. Middle age and the years beyond loom like a vast and scary unknown. How will I navigate my parents' aging, my own aging, my daughter's life changes—all of it—without a partner? Everyone I know has a partner. Everyone. It's what I have been taught to look for my whole life, and after failing miserably a few times along the way, I finally have a traditional family unit. I am no longer the weird single mom at my daughter's school: we are a two-income, upper-middle-class trio, a family like almost all of the other families. And every family has its problems, right?

The idea of being single again in my 40s is extra cringy. It's too late to start over in a new relationship, with all the shit that involves: having to get to know someone new, deal with their baggage, learn to be intimate with them, let them enter the complexities of my family life. How exhausting. And as a divorcee two times over already, my prospects of finding a decent guy were already low when my husband and I got together. Imagine being divorced *three* times? That makes me practically Liz Taylor, without the violet eyes. And as my husband likes to remind me often, no one will want a woman who has been married and divorced three times: "Good luck trying to find someone to love you now, Nicole," he laughed the last time talk of divorce surfaced.

No. I am stubbornly determined to make this marriage work, determined to make him want me and want the lifestyle I have always imagined for us—a lifestyle he insists he wants and that he *sometimes* embraces. The fact that he sometimes wants it makes me hold on to the hope that one day he will *always* want it.

"YO!" My father's booming greeting fills the front porch and interrupts my train of self-pity.

"What?"

"D.F.R." He looks at me, pointing his thumb in the direction of the bay and the bridge that leads off the island. "Down the Fucking Road with this guy."

"But Dad—"

"I know you don't want to hear it. But let me tell you something. Sometimes you're in the end zone and you have to decide if you're gonna run or pass the ball. And sometimes you wanna run, but you gotta pass the ball."

Or something like that.

My father, the football coach, often gives life advice in football plays.

"Okay..."

"You know, it's enough already. Your mother's giving me goddamned agita over this every day. Enough. Let him go. D.F.R."

Big Nick certainly raised me to be my own person, warning me never to let myself become dependent on anyone. I am ashamed of myself as I wallow in the failure of another marriage. Where is that independent woman now, and who is this dependent, spineless doormat in her place?

My father's ultimatum is understandable. The last time I was at the shore for a weekend away, about a year ago, my husband told me not to bother coming home. I did anyway, and he stayed in bed all weekend with pillows over his head, refusing to even look at me. He pulled away even more into his life away from home and was gone more than he was home. When he was home, he was drunk more than he was sober. He kept saying I was the reason. He told his friends I wouldn't let him go out anymore, and consequently, they stopped speaking to me. I was a controlling shrew. I was the problem. "All my friends hate you," he said, "they keep telling me to leave you. I don't know why I don't listen to them."

Feeling like everything was my fault, I sank deeper and deeper into self-loathing. I tried hard to make him want me. When I look back on the lengths to which I went—changing hairstyles, wearing more makeup, buying pretty clothes, doing everything he wanted to do (even sexually) to keep him, I am disgusted with myself.

At the end of last summer, I discovered on his Facebook messenger, which he had displayed on his open laptop on the dining room table, that he was sexting with a woman I had suspected he was getting too close to for months. *I had a dirty dream about you... You and I would have great sex!* My heart stopped. We were married. All my efforts to keep him, and nothing worked. He still wanted someone else.

Compounding my hurt and anger over the sexting incident was the rolled-up bill with the powder-dusted ends I found in his pants pocket while I was sorting through the dirty laundry after he returned from a "business trip." That was enough. I would not have drugs in my house, especially around my pre-teen daughter.

In a huge emotional meltdown that brought my parents across the driveway to help me, I kicked him out. He was gone for almost three months. I initiated divorce proceedings. I had a lot of explaining to do to my daughter, who had found out about my husband's cocaine use from a text his brother had sent to her—"accidentally"—and had come home from her dad's weekend to the news that my husband was no longer living with us.

And as for my husband's infidelity...I had no idea how far it had gone, but I learned from someone that while I was on a service trip overseas with students that summer, he was at the Belmont Stakes with the woman, and they had shared a hotel room. It was more than I could bear. And yet, I took him back.

As angry and hurt as I was, I felt like I had failed as a wife—failed to make my husband happy, so that he had to look elsewhere. And I missed him. I missed the good times we had together, and I missed the man who made me laugh.

It turned out he missed me, too. He texted me right before Thanksgiving to say he wanted to work things out. He promised me he would never use drugs again. It was only one time, he swore, and the sexting was a stupid mistake that he never intended to follow through on. They only had "an inappropriate friendship," he insisted. He was drunk when he sent the messages to her. And, anyway, angry with me because I was still in contact with an ex-boyfriend—a man I had known for 25 years who lived and worked on another continent. That didn't matter, my husband said. He was convinced I was still in love with the ex. That his side relationship was a response to my own "inappropriate friendship" with my ex.

He told me he would come home under two conditions: we would get a marriage counselor, and I would stop all communication with my ex. I told him no drugs, no drunkenness, and no other women. He promised he would not drink at home. In fact, he said, if I ended my friendship with my ex-boyfriend, he would never do any of that again. He would only want me. He would be faithful from now on. He would come home and be around more often. He would stop drinking completely. He would stop talking to this other woman. All of our problems, he said, hinged on his anger over my friendship with my ex.

The easy solution was for me to end the friendship. I didn't want to. I didn't like the way he used it to justify his own bad choices. But I felt somehow responsible for the mess our marriage had become, and guilty that I had caused all of our problems; I had brought everything on myself over a friendship with a man I hadn't seen in years. So, I promised my husband I would end the friendship. I wrote the ex-boyfriend and told him I was sorry, but my husband found our friendship inappropriate and we couldn't be friends anymore. I cried for a week over it.

And then, against my parents' strong advice, I welcomed my husband home. We started working with a therapist. He wasn't using cocaine, at least as far as I knew. He became more involved in my daughter's life, and she seemed happy that he was his fun old self again with us. Things were good until late spring, and then...we wound up here.

———

But this time, even though I am trying hard to establish what my therapist and our marriage counselor call "boundaries," I am worried. It hits me around mid-morning that he had admitted acting on a suicide threat. Holy shit. What if he went through with it? What if he were dead, and here I am sitting on a chaise lounge?

I text him before lunch, and receive only: *I'm fine, don't text me again. And don't come home. We're done.* Throughout the day, he is posting photos of himself out and about in the city, seeming, at least according to Facebook, to be having a great time. No evidence of the alleged suicide attempt. Had it been a cry for help, or a drunken display of drama on his part?

In the end, after calling my therapist, who tells me the best thing I can do now is take care of myself and my daughter, I resign myself to accept that there is nothing I can do but let him go and protect myself from whatever force is creating this latest storm in him. The police had determined he wasn't in danger, and he outright stated he didn't want to see me. He had made choices. He is a grown man. I am confused, hurt, angry, but most of all, emotionally exhausted. Plus, though I hate to admit what seems like defeat, I know, in my heart, my father is right. I never should have taken him back the last time.

I stay at the shore.

My daughter, who is in Colorado with her father and his parents for a few weeks, calls for her daily check-in, and I don't say anything to her about the suicide attempt or the fact that we are probably actually getting a divorce this time. I have to process things myself before I can present them properly to her—which is pretty much how I have been handling my family: I have become a PR agent for my marriage to everyone around me.

———

Two days after my husband's suicide attempt, he texts me: *I moved out. Good luck.*

He had told me not to come home until he moved out. I stay a few more days at the shore to prepare myself to face whatever would come next. We go straight no-contact.

"Don't worry," my mom says. "It's going to be ok. You have us and your sister. We will help you."

"Thanks, Mom."

I am too old to be taken care of by my parents. This marriage was my last chance to make my own family. Last chance saloon. That keeps running through my head. And now I am alone in the dirt road among the tumbleweeds of midlife.

At the end of the week, defeated and facing the gaping void of the second half of my life alone, I pack the car and head north toward home on the Garden State Parkway.

While I am driving home from the shore, he calls me, and I almost don't pick up. As his name flashes above the odometer and the phone screams through the Bluetooth, I tell myself I am seriously done with his manipulation and bullshit. I can do this on my own. Why should I pick up and deal with whatever emotionally charged shit he has decided he needs to throw at me today?

When he calls again, I cave. My father always taught me to be independent. My parents pushed me to become educated so that I could always take care of myself. I took him back once before, and our marriage didn't magically transform into the partnership I wanted. Yet, I am tired. When we got together, my husband seemed solid, someone I could lean on when adulting was difficult.

And now, here I am, emotionally dependent on a man who can't take care of me, having to relearn how to be independent at mid-life.

I push the "answer" button on the steering wheel. And his voice this morning seems different from the other several times he's asked to come home after one of his manic, drunken binges, when he recently started to interpret my stipulation of do not come home drunk as do not come home if you want to get drunk—stay out and get drunk for days.

He is in tears. "Please help me," he begs. "I need help and I can't help myself." He tells me that he has again thought about suicide, this time contemplating throwing himself in front of the Acela— timing its speeding journey past the station where he catches the train to work each morning. He almost did it, too. He is scared and out of control in a way that I've never heard him before.

"I'm losing my mind," he says. "Do not leave me alone in this city." I am driving toward home, trying to focus on the road and not on the frantic voice coming through the Bluetooth from an entire state away. A voice deep inside me tells me this is the moment to call one of his brothers and let them deal with him. That this kind of life is not good for my daughter or myself. But my heart tells me this is the man I married. The man whom I had called my best friend in front of everyone in the Meeting House on our wedding day, almost exactly three years ago to the date. He needs me.

Despite all of our fights and the terrible things he'd said to me, despite the fact that he has left me, has not held his end of the bargain, and has more than once this summer blown through all of our money for the month on partying, karaoke nights with colleagues, and drinking binges, I say, "Ask for a medical leave of absence from work and come home. I will take care of you." He does. He comes home.

I drive him to the mental health crisis center, where we are processed and searched in every room, with everything on display for the guards and nurses, including my wedding and engagement rings in the little velvet box that holds them both, side-by-side, the way he had presented them to me when he proposed. Days earlier, in one of his nastygrams, he'd demanded I remove them because they were "lies" around my finger. They are still in my purse when we are searched.

"Your rings," he says sadly.

"You demanded I remove them," I snap.

The intake nurse and security guard keep their eyes down, but I notice a sideways glance between them. I wonder how many of these relationships they've seen and how many couples actually stay together after this kind of night.

Behind the third locked door, in the intake room, I sit alone on a hard plastic couch. My husband has been taken to a room to be evaluated, and I am not permitted beyond this room with the orange plastic couches. I am the only one in the room, except for a guard who sits overlooking the space from a booth made of a thick sheet of hard plastic. The weather channel is on the television; major storms lurk over the area. Big red blobs indicating violent weather cover the various counties on the map. My phone doesn't have service, and I have nothing to read. All I can do is watch those storms overtake the city on the TV screen—and wait.

The man I love is still there, somewhere, underneath the anger, the stress, the frustration with our marriage. That guy who, with a flourish, can open two car doors at the same time. The guy who loves 80s music, quirky comedies, and the beach as much as I do. The guy who was the Napoleon to my Madonna at our first Halloween together. The guy who bought me a laptop to replace the one that was stolen when my house was robbed before we were married. The guy who calls me "Lover," which always makes me smile. The guy who loves being seen at fancy places and dressing up to the nines with me. When things are going well between us, we make a great pair. I want that guy back, and I am determined not to lose him.

The red storm warning is now flashing on the screen, and the whole city is on high alert for severe thunderstorms and tornadoes. A few minutes before, the red blobs were circling the city; now we are fully inundated.

How did things go so badly so quickly? How did I not see the warning signs in my own marriage?

In the cold loneliness of that crisis center waiting room, our terrible fights start to make sense. They seem to be part of a larger problem that perhaps I somehow have a hand in solving, starting with my picking up the phone that morning. The manic episodes, followed by the lows that drive him to bed for days. The accusations. The suicidal ideation. Maybe there was a medical reason behind all of it, and this is our chance to fix it. It makes perfect sense. Why else would a wonderful man act so terribly?

I feel a tiny spark of hope as I sit there and watch some of the red storm splotches turn to green and then clear out of the area. It seems symbolic—like a sign from the universe that things will be okay. Maybe the psychiatrist on duty will change the dosage of the anti-anxiety medication our family doctor had given him to help with work stress, tell him to stop drinking so much, and that's all it will take. Maybe this time it will work out. I am hopeful. The storm warning passes, and the nurse opens the door, ushering me through to the room where my husband is waiting.

———

He is admitted to the Dual Diagnosis Unit, in a behavioral health hospital. His issues have a name: Major Depressive Disorder and Self-Medication with Substances.

I follow behind the ambulance that transports him to the hospital. Through the rainy windshield and the windows on the back of the vehicle, I see him, a vague form on a stretcher. I feel that somehow this is the end of a long struggle—no matter what happens at that hospital, my life, and his, will change. Maybe we will stay together, maybe not. I have no answers, and my heart is empty of all emotion for the first time in years.

———

When my husband comes home from the hospital, everything feels different. I, of course, am optimistic that the darkness has been removed from our lives for good. He has been "fixed," he says on the drive home. Everything is going to be fine now.

My parents are watching from their living room windows but do not come out to say hello when we pull up to the house. They are worried, and they fear for my safety and my daughter's safety. I've had to convince them it was ok for him to come home. That he was going to stop drinking and partying, that he was taking new medication—the right medication this time—and that he would be seeing a therapist, not just our marriage counselor, but his own therapist. He has a diagnosed illness, I explained. And a lot of work stress. He's not a bad person; he just didn't have the right kind of treatment before. As long as he took his medication and saw his doctor, he would be fine. Everything would be as we always wanted it to be. We'd have barbecues, badminton matches in the backyard, nice summers at the shore—all the time, like we had had periodically when things were good between us.

My father was skeptical about the whole thing. "You know, these people never change," he warned. "I've seen it first-hand."

"No, Dad, the doctors said he would be ok," I told him. "We have a whole team of people to help him manage his illness. It's going to work out this time."

He shrugged. "Well, I'm just telling you. He has problems that will never go away."

T. Nicole Cirone is the author of Nine Nails: A Novel in Essays *(Serving House Books, 2019). She is an editor at* The Night Heron Barks *and* Ran Off With the Star Bassoon. *Her works have been published in* Ovunque Siamo, Serving House Journal, Philadelphia Stories, The Woman Inc., Hippocampus, Red River Review, Bucks Country Writer, *the* Philadelphia Stories *"Best of" Anthology,* Gateways:

An Anthology, *and* Reading Beyond the Saguaros: A Prosimetric Travelogue. *She holds degrees from Rosemont College (Bachelor of Arts Degrees in Italian Studies and Political Science, and a Master of Arts in Literature and Writing), and a dual concentration Master of Fine Arts in Creative Writing (poetry and CNF) from Fairleigh Dickinson University. Cirone is currently a graduate student in the Human Sexuality program at Widener University. She is a high school English teacher, a university writing instructor, a yoga instructor, a mom, and a cat mom. Instagram:* @catmumu123.

Dual Diagnosis *is excerpted from* Nine Nails: A Novel in Essays *(Serving House Books, 2019) and is printed with permission.*

Not All Love Can

Amanda Stevens-Loper

Sometimes, you show up as a bunch of mismatched pieces held together with paperclips and rubber bands. You're not where you want to be, but you don't know how to leave this place. It's not comfortable, but it's familiar.

The right person will see you for your chaos and meet you where you are. They'll squint and tilt their heads, letting their eyes slide out of focus, constructing a concept of who you'll be once the cracks are cemented. A concept of who you were before things got so heavy. A concept of who you are, if only you had the strength right now.

But you don't have the strength. You're tired all the way to your bones. You're weary, spent, trudging under the weight of your choices and your circumstances. The burden is unrelenting and it pushes you further down, stooping your back and blunting your mind.

They'll invite you to show up with that weight. They'll take your baggage. Not to unpack it, but to just let it be. They'll help you take inventory of it, their fingers sliding painfully and deliberately along weathered suitcases and tarnished latches. They'll add their own to the pile: tattered boxes, dusty trunks, overstuffed suitcases. Some fall open where they are dropped, but some are held shut with heavy locks. You don't know the combination, but they're not yours to open.

You'll sit there, the two of you, in the shadow cast by your heaping pile of *stuff* in the sickly yellow porch light. The old boards whine under the weight. It's an oddly fitting sound.

You'll share a cigarette and a bottle of wine. It doesn't matter that he doesn't smoke. It doesn't matter that you don't like merlot. You don't talk. You just sit, inhaling the quiet and the cancer, the crackling of the tobacco warming the snowy night.

You're safe, so you tell him things you've never told anyone. You hand him your dreams, your fears and your insecurities. He'll patch up what he can and you'll be strong enough to carry on from there. While you're fighting yourself, he'll hold you together. Like you have before, you will love him. For the first time, though, you will let someone see you. You will let someone love you.

It doesn't last forever, though, because not all love does. Pay attention to the way his hand warms yours, keeping you steady. Hold on to the way he kisses you hello, no matter how long you've been apart, and the way he smooths your hair against the pillow when he leaves in the morning. Remember the way his laugh echoes on empty streets at two a.m., and the way he folds you into his life, and the way he lets you be vulnerable. The way he's proud to be seen with you. The way he moves closer to you as he falls asleep. The way it feels to be riding in a convertible, half-drunk, at one o'clock on Christmas morning.

Take all of that…and add it to your baggage. It's all yours now, even though he isn't. That love will slip through your fingers, fragile and glimmering, as you turn away. Pack up your stuff, wave into the rearview mirror and push forward.

What you're moving toward is beautiful. The next time, someone will unpack and purge with you. They'll help you evaluate what to keep and what to leave.

You'll realize that you're missing some stuff, though, and you've taken some things that aren't yours. He's kept some of your blockade, the one that kept you safe from people and kept people safe from you. You've kept just a little bit of his pain and his anger and the part of him that can't go to work every day.

And you will hold onto those things for each other. Not all love lasts forever, because not all love can.

———

Amanda Stevens-Loper has been an avid reader since kindergarten and maintains a passion for all things written. Though she is a native New Yorker, she currently lives in San Antonio with her husband, two small children, two big dogs and an old cat. She collects antique books and the gem of her collection was printed in 1726! This is her first published work. She is so incredibly grateful for both those who encouraged her to submit her work and those who provided the inspiration.

Rebel by Nature (and Probably Nurture): A Story of a Mental Health Therapist

Terri Parke

I was born the second of three children in a family of five. I am the second girl, born twenty-three months after my older sister. My brother came along three and a half years later.

Some of my earliest memories involve arguing with family members, particularly my sister. She and I loved to argue about the forthcoming addition to the family.

"She's going to be a girl, and her name should be Crystal," I said, smiling and doing a little twirl. I love to dance. I like to get my way and tend to smile as a first attempt.

As for the name Crystal, I liked that name, and I wanted someone to boss around just like my older sister bossed me. Or maybe I wanted to lead them, as leading is something I really like to do in almost any circumstance.

I can remember standing in argument with her, she who had a great grasp of vocabulary from a young age and is just about as strong-willed as I am, if not more.

"No. I told you. We already have two girls. We need a brother. And his name isn't going to be Crystal, that's a girl's name."

Little did we know, his name would be Michael. That is my dad's name, and my mom's favorite name. It was also a very common name during the early seventies.

As I got older and wished I had a more feminine name, I learned that all three of us would have been named Michael, with different middle names.

In Texas, where I live, people tend to call me Teresa, but I prefer going by Terri. A few years ago, someone told me I was one of the 'lucky' ones who had a name without gender. Let me tell you, that has not been my feeling about having a name that can be both masculine and feminine. I can remember searching for trinkets with the name 'Terri' on them. I could sometimes find 'Terry,' which is the masculine version and not how I spell my name. It was a pretty special occasion when my mom or I located one with my name and spelled correctly.

I came out a little oppositional. My due date was in late August, and I was born in mid-September. Opposition means going against. There's an author I follow (Gretchen Ruben) who describes four personality types, and one of them is coined *rebel*.

To be oppositional, or rebellious, or saying 'no' just because someone told you to do something, are all very similar words for a similar behavioral tendency.

It is not just saying no because someone said yes. It is more than just disagreeing with a proposed plan. It is saying the sky is purple because someone else said it was blue, but also with a little 'kick' to it. A little sass, a little emphasis, a little more rebelliousness.

I am a second-born child, second girl before the boy. I have high energy and I love to move. My brain likes to make quick connections, has quite a lot of working memory, and I put a high value on communicating verbally and visually.

I am strong-willed, nurtured in a family of origin with and by other strong-willed people.

I have grown up watching my parents direct and lead, as my dad taught middle and high school band students within my school system. My mom taught choir and music in a neighboring school corporation (district) and county.

My parents grew up in urban Indianapolis, living not too far away from each other. They met at Butler University where they both participated in marching band. Prior to that, my dad attended and graduated from a private high school named Cathedral. My mom attended the local public school system, Arsenal Technical High School.

Both my parents worked outside of our hometown, and this distance was starting to make life complicated. They talked about moving to Tipton, Indiana, but it was a difficult choice for my mom. Not only would they have to adjust to living in a rural community, but also it would mean she'd be farther away from her mom. The local phone call Mom and Grandma had grown accustomed to sharing practically every day would become a toll call, and the thirty-minute drive to visit each other would become a full hour.

As a kid, I can remember listening to my parents negotiate how my mom would maintain the close relationship she had with her mom. Hearing her worry about being able to see and visit Grandma instilled in me the importance of family and friends. To this day, I put high value on those special relationships.

After we moved to Tipton, my mom worked hard to establish friendships for herself and for the family unit as we got involved in a local church close to our house. She had to work hard because the community was already tightly knit, made up of people who had grown up together—families and friends—for years and years. Living such short distances from other family members is the norm for people from Tipton. I can remember how surprised my friends and their parents were that even though I had a lot of cousins, none of them lived in Tipton.

I was able to continue to have a close relationship with my grandma no matter where we lived. Each of us kids got to spend our own special week each summer with her, and sometimes all the siblings visited at once. These visits allowed my mom some extra quiet time at home.

As we got close to the start of kindergarten, I had one thought in mind: I just wanted to be around people my age.

As fate would have it, our house sold in July, 1976. We moved our things to our new home in Tipton with the smooth sidewalks for roller skating, where we would have a short walk to school. We looked at several houses, but I wanted to be able to roller skate.

In addition to the events of moving school districts and homes, or possibly in the midst of moving, there was a local, tragic death of a middle school student who was watching his sister. He touched an electrical wire and did not survive. Some of my first memories of living in Tipton involve the events surrounding that funeral, as the eighth grader was the son of one of my parents' friends, and my mom helped to care for the children during the funeral. They also had a child who was preparing at that time to begin kindergarten, and we are friends to this day.

We had moved to a relatively quiet street in Tipton, where people were discouraged from driving down it by the stop signs that occurred at every single intersection. Our comment of "Look! We can cross the street without even looking here!" was not received as well following my friend's brother's death. It was a definite shift from our in-town home in Noblesville, which was really, really close to the Boys and Girls Club and had quite a bit more traffic.

—

Since I moved to McKinney, Texas, in 2019, I have been particularly interested and fascinated by the number of cultures and ethnicities represented here in this city, which is the county seat of Collin County.

We have been here almost two years now, with one of them being a full year plus of the pandemic. Being social, but also introverted (or a shy extrovert, I'm not sure which ones applies, other than I think they are probably the same), I find myself wanting the same things I had wanted when I was five and beginning school. I am looking forward to meeting people and getting to know them in person rather than virtually.

I have noticed in the last few weeks, since vaccines have become more common and people have begun to come out of their homes and be a little more social, the excitement I felt at five of being able to get to know people and establish friendships is the same.

Here, instead of being the person from Tipton who works in Noblesville and surrounding counties, I am an empty nester from Indiana.

People have described me as someone 'without any accent at all,' which I find fairly interesting. My friendly nature is liked and appreciated by some, while others tend to veer away.

I live on a street and community with lots of different cultures and ethnicities. We are close to multiple businesses that have moved their home offices from California to Texas, and we live in an area that was a field not too terribly long ago.

I'm getting to know neighbors and friends who are from Texas, Columbia, Venezuela, China, India, New York, Tennessee, and so many more places.

I am able to provide mental health therapy at a time when the stigma is really being reduced. I work primarily with teens, parents, and those with attention, anxiety, or depressive tendencies.

It's an exciting time to be a part of this field, which I entered formally in 1995 when I graduated with my degree in Community Counseling. I get to hear parents tell me that they are bringing their teens to therapy because the teens asked for it for many years. I get to meet with adults who have very little background in being in tune with their feelings, and report of feeling better from mental health therapy but not really knowing why.

I exercised some of my rebelliousness when I chose my university and my career back in the early 90s. My mom, dad, multiple aunts, sister, and brother all went to Butler. I didn't want to attend Butler, so I applied to Indiana University in Bloomington.

Indiana University is a large, Big 10 University. The size made my parents hesitant, as they were comfortable with a small university like Butler. I went into the field of mental health, which I would say I was born to do and pursued from an early age.

And boy, am I glad I did.

— ⁓ —

Terri Parke graduated from Indiana University with a Bachelor of Science in Psychology, and the University of Cincinnati with a Masters of Arts in Community Counseling. Terri grew up in Indiana, and moved to Texas in 2019, just nine months prior to the COVID pandemic. She grew up working in the corn fields, which is a far cry from where she lives now.

She loves to take pictures, chat with friends, and write about subjects that interest her.

Terri has worked much of her career in the nonprofit sector, and also provides mental health therapy in an outpatient setting. She primarily focuses on patients with attention, depressive, and anxiety tendencies, as well as those who have experienced trauma.

Terri likes to write about trauma, mental health issues, and other topics that interest her. She maintains a blog at www.terriswritings.com. She has twin twenty-something sons, and lives in McKinney with her husband Matt and their dog Mosby. She is getting used to being an empty nester, tends to be overly optimistic, and loves Pilates.

HOW TO PROCESS FEELINGS IN AN ABUSIVE RELATIONSHIP

Gurpreet Dhariwal

Trigger Warning: this article contains descriptions of domestic violence and abuse that may not be suitable for all readers. Fearless community, please read with care.

Has he ever trapped you in a room and not let you out?
Has he ever raised a fist as if he were going to hit you?
Has he ever thrown an object that hit you or nearly did?
Has he ever held you down or grabbed you to restrain you?
Has he ever shoved, poked, or grabbed you?
Has he ever threatened to hurt you?
If the answer to any of these questions is yes, then we can stop wondering whether he'll ever be violent; he already has been.
— Lundy Bancroft

In the year 2015, I got married with my consent, which is not always the case in India. It was a love marriage. A few weeks before the wedding, several arguments and fights took place and I stepped back from marrying him. I didn't entertain him and his greedy family for a week. Then, not realizing the gravity of the situation,

I told myself that things would change after marriage and went ahead with the wedding. I was wrong, and I had to pay the price.

Nothing changed. I started to understand that you either accept and surrender to the bullshit or live under the illusion that everything will eventually be alright and work out.

My husband started hitting me within three weeks of our marriage. When I retaliated, he hit me more.

To everyone out there, man or woman, going through a similar struggle: I know it can feel like the world has halted for an eternity. But I'm here to share with you the obstacles that I faced and how I overcame them.

The first obstacle was accepting the truth that I was no longer in a happy marriage.

So what if it was a love marriage. It was hell for me.

How did I accept it?

After posting pictures on social media and earning supportive praises from loved ones, I concluded that I was in a shitty marriage.

I wasn't seeking social media assurance and acceptance, but that support helped me understand I'd been ignoring the shit in my head. I finally realized my marriage gave me severe depression, anxiety, and suicidal thoughts—but not happiness.

Acceptance of my situation helped me to figure out that the status of my marriage was negatively affecting my mental health.

The second obstacle was deciding on whom to trust with my story.

I was in pain and I was seeking validation.

How did I stop seeking validation?

I didn't open much about myself and my marriage with my friends in the initial months. I was sure they wouldn't get it because they were regular visitors on my social media channels and they thought everything was alright.

But some people don't understand that everything online is not the entire truth. Some of us live in the confinements of our minds. I opened up with my best friend, and while I was thinking he understood my issues, I saw his comments on the same topic in an amusing manner. I realized he was sicker than I was. I stopped seeking validation of my miseries, and it helped me a lot.

The third obstacle was making a plan to leave my bastard husband.

I wanted to leave him, and I did in my head.

How did I face it?

My husband was an insane, shithead soul. He always raised hands to me and treated me like a piece of shit. I had to find a way to save myself. It was after a year I realized that I had already left him in my head long ago.

What I used to feel for him wasn't hate, but I did pity him. I wish somebody could have helped him to not repeat the same mistakes that he'd learned from his father.

Even though we lived separately from his parents after ten months of marriage living without them, I saw the same rage in his eyes. He always thought that he was teaching me a lesson, but I knew how weak he was as a human to take out his frustration on me when I didn't deserve it.

Leaving him mentally made me strong enough to leave him physically.

The fourth obstacle was giving him more time than he deserved to file for the mutually consented divorce.

I knew he wouldn't agree, but still I waited.

How did I respond to it?

I received papers from my husband asking for a divorce in December 2017. I waited for six months for him to take the papers back so that we could head for the mutual divorce. He never agreed to a mutual divorce and considered it as a sign of weakness from my end. But I wasn't a weak soul then, nor am I today.

After seeing his insane attitude, I filed for divorce on the grounds of domestic violence and pressed dowry charges. His parents had abused me when I was living with them, and after ten months of marriage when I was forced to leave their abode, they abused me in my rented apartment, too.

I didn't bow down. I took charge of my situation. I am now fighting my case with utmost sincerity and dignity. He will have to pay for the damage he caused me.

———

Hear this domestic violence advice loud and clear:

Coming out of domestic violence where you have been abused all day and night is not an easy game. Some people will show you sympathy without realizing it's not what you need the most. Some people will listen to your stories just to ditch you later. Some people will be nice to your face and ruin everything behind your back with false stories.

But you've got to understand one thing. You aren't moving out of your marriage because of society, the world, or your family members. You're doing it for yourself—just like the way I have done it for myself.

The journey will be ruthless and will threaten to break your spirit, but I realized God wouldn't lead me astray. People do. I put God first and saw the courage I got in return from the universe.

———

Professional Guidance for Others Suffering from Domestic Violence and Abuse

If you are currently in an abusive relationship:
- Tell someone you trust
- Ask for help in case you need to leave
- Identify a location where you will go
- Pack a bag that will not be missed and hide it in a safe place or keep it with someone you trust

Pack your bag with:
- Mobile phone
- Cash (including coins for phone calls) and checks

- Clothes and personal items for you and your children (such as a special toy or book)
- Medications
- House and car keys
- Important phone numbers

In addition, be sure to pack copies of important papers, including:
- Your driver's license or another picture ID
- Birth certificates
- Passports
- Health insurance information
- House and car titles
- Rent receipts
- Your marriage license
- Your children's immunization records

After you leave an abusive relationship, you must protect yourself:
- Change your home and/or mobile phone numbers, and screen calls
- Keep a record of all contacts, messages, injuries, and other incidents involving the abuser
- Change the locks if the abuser has a key
- Plan how to get away if confronted by the abuser
- Notify school and work contacts so they can protect you and your children
- If you have to meet your abusive partner, do it in public

The National Domestic Violence Hotline has counselors who can provide help in 170 languages. They can give you information about local resources. Visit the link below for more information:

My Doctor Online - mydoctor.kaiserpermanente.org

Now let's move on to the subject of how a real man treats his wife. A real man doesn't slap even a ten-dollar hooker around, if he's got any self-respect, much less hurt his own woman. Much less ten times over the mother of his kids. A real man busts his ass to feed his family, fights for them if he has to, dies for them if he has to. And he treats his wife with respect every day of his life, treats her like a queen — the queen of the home she makes for their children.

— **S.M. Stirling**

Gurpreet Dhariwal is addicted to writing, reading, painting, feeding stray dogs, solo traveling, and bike rides. Her debut poetry book, My Soul Rants: Poems of a Born Spectator, was published in 2020 and got her appreciation and accolades from people all over the world. She published her second poetry book Kaurageously Yours in 2021.

Gurpreet firmly believes in karma philosophy and humanity. Her poetry reflects the poignant situations that are neglected at large in a hypocritical society. Between monotonous daily routines, she has been writing two books, and one of them is set on her own journey of domestic violence survival.

She gives a damn how the world perceives her as it took her a great deal to wear her scars on her sleeve and accept her flaws as strengths. Her world revolves in and around books and she is an avid reader. She travels to places she reads about, makes friends with the characters, falls in love, and fights with demons she gets to face every day in people.

She has double master's degrees in Information Technology and Computer Applications. She found her bliss in writing when she was eighteen years old. Currently, she resides in Delhi, India, with her parents.

You can read more about her at the following links:
https://www.gurpreetdhariwal.com
https://www.facebook.com/authorgurpreetdhariwal/

https://www.instagram.com/authorgurpreetdhariwal/
https://twitter.com/authorgurpreetd
https://www.linkedin.com/in/authorgurpreetdhariwal/
https://www.medium.com/@dhariwalgurpreet

FOLLOWING THE CURRENT

Giana Hesterberg

Growing up along the Texas Gulf Coast, South Padre Island was a favorite family destination. Now an adult raising my own children in the same area, I can't seem to apply Banana Boat sunscreen—the one in the plastic, orange container—without being transported to the beach.

Visions of my toes in the sand, my hands clenching a bologna-and-cheese sandwich inside a Ziploc bag, rush in. I wasn't the biggest fan of bologna, but that mattered little when the ocean fed my hunger. Eating sandwiches is boring these days, unless they're accompanied by wind, waves, and a hint of sand for that extra crunch.

Getting from the car to the water was sometimes challenging, depending on what time we arrived at the beach. My rubber flip flops did a poor job protecting my toes and the sides of my feet from the scorching hot, soft sand. I seldom carried anything out to sea as a child, save for my sand toys. Once we arrived at the perfect mix of hard and soft, we set out a Mexican *serape* blanket, black and white in color, held down in one corner by a red ice chest with a white lid. We removed our sandals and set them down on opposite ends.

My petite mom typically wore a black bikini, her tan skin at home by the water, but not in it. Book in hand and lying on the opposite arm, she preferred reading with one eye open, the other shut, under her half-moon shaped lenses. Her right ankle rested on her left knee, creating a small triangle. Short, dark hair framed her face and almond-shaped eyes, with a smile as bright as sunshine.

My stepdad *was* the water, constantly fishing or swimming in it. His hair matched the sand, and his green eyes the seaweed. With a long, lean build, his layered bronze skin was achieved after years of not wearing sunblock. My parents were like the ocean, constantly moving and never still, with loud, crashing sounds, rushing forward and receding.

A few times we ventured to the end of the island, Isla Blanca Park, and paid a ten-dollar fee to access the children's beach. The children's beach was not an ideal spot for me. Sprinkled with hundreds of seashells, I passed the time avoiding them with my feet and following my parents on a path along the jetties—gigantic rocks that line a side of the ocean. Seawater splashed and seeped through the large, gaping holes.

One particular morning, my mother and I built two small sand mounds joined by a bridge made out of twigs and dried up seaweed. After playing in the water, we returned to find a little boy leaving our creation, a smashed bridge in his wake, his small feet trailing pieces of my shattered soul. I was a sensitive child and no stranger to imagination. Many years passed before I began to understand that the bridge that exists between a mother and daughter is one that needs occasional maintenance. And it was a few years later that the seagulls of sadness would threaten to build homes in our family's hearts.

The end of a trip to the Gulf Coast was typically anticlimactic. After rinsing off in the public showers, plastic gallon jugs filled with seawater were used to rinse off our feet and sandals. This became a permanent part of the exiting process in my mind. I was reminded of this meaningful tradition when twenty-six-year-old me visited the beach with my future husband and his family. My boyfriend had knelt down to gently pour water on my feet as I sat at the back of his parents' Suburban, and I knew he would be my anchor. This small act paralleled Jesus washing his disciples' feet and I was sold. Here was a man who would spend his life serving me. My season of longing for love and companionship was over.

An image of my newly-minted fiancé and me, embracing on the jetties while my younger sister snapped a photo of us, seconds before a massive wave threatened to throw her tiny body out to sea, makes me smile. Our grins were never bigger, and our bodies never thinner.

Our Texas beach continues to be my favorite spot in the world. When I had lived in landlocked Iowa for seven years, a state that is gorgeous in its own way, I yearned for the smell of salt. *Let's go to the beach*, friends said. Confused but cautiously optimistic, I obliged. Where is this beach and how long will it take to get there? I quietly wondered in the backseat of a vehicle.

We arrived at Red Rock Lake in Pella, Iowa, with "sand" by the water as proof. I put on a good face but was disappointed. This is not a beach, was all I thought.

I would try, on more than one occasion, to mold myself into an Iowan—my salty waves conforming to rigid rows of corn. Before moving back to Texas and meeting my future husband, I thought I might marry a farmer and live there forever. I had no particular farmer in mind; I only wanted land. Then I met multiple farming families and learned of their hardships and thought better of it. Moving back to the Gulf Coast, as much as I loved it, took some convincing. If you look closely, you can still see my reluctant finger marks on the large stretch of I-35 heading south.

When I ran away from home at the ripe age of eighteen—not literally, under the guise of *going off to college*—I had no plans of returning. There were few good qualities about my border town of Brownsville, unspoken evils I closely bore witness to: absentee fathers, drug abuse, corruption, and oppressive *machismo* culture. Anywhere else was going to be better. The world was mine and I was an oyster, with a built-up rough exterior, nearly impossible to open, unaware that I possessed any pearls. I clung to anything that held a hint of familiarity, an underlying current of *you're not going to leave me too, are you?*

When I was fourteen, I was diagnosed with *Pityriasis Lichenoides Chronica* (PLC), a skin condition that appears like multiple, bright red bug bites on the skin. Though it was a mild life-long sentence, my adolescent mind exacerbated the problem. *Everyone can see it and it's gross*, furthering the unworthy narrative that had etched itself into my soul. To make up for it, I had a loud, bubbly exterior that overflowed onto everything I touched. I was too much for some, claiming that the volume of my boisterous personality hurt their sensitive ears and egos.

I was never too much for the Clarks. Tall, blonde-haired and blue-eyed with glasses, I met the twins my sophomore year of high school in history class. The connection was instantaneous, confirmed the moment we discussed our birthdays: the three of us were born in the same hospital, in the same city, on the same day, December 29, 1981, and I was born right smack between them! Ryan arrived at 11:11 pm, I arrived at 11:29 pm, and Andrew was delivered at 11:46 pm. From that moment on, we were soulmates.

We drove the twenty minutes out to the beach one summer day, *The Cars Greatest Hits* in my cassette player. Because I was comfortable with them, I wore a swimsuit and shorts. Upon arriving, we quickly made our way out to the water. I was careful to make sure I was in deep enough to disguise the PLC on my short legs.

As we all splashed around, I noticed one of my legs poking out and quickly hid it. Andrew looked at me, confused. "I don't want you to see my skin problem," I confessed.

He grabbed my leg out of the water with his large hand, and looked directly at me, saying, "Hey, you're beautiful." He became my gold standard after that, the person by which I would subconsciously rank all other friends and future suitors.

The Clarks were true Eagle Scouts—natural leaders, poised to help at a moment's notice, chivalrous, smart, and funny. My stepdad would tell me, on more than one occasion, "You should be more like your twin friends." My mother was convinced one of them would ask for my hand in marriage one day.

Life is often like waves in the ocean, with its unpredictable ebb and flow, moments preserved in the soul, others washed away. The Clarks married within one year of each other—naturally—immediately after we all graduated from college. I flew down to Texas from Iowa for each of their nuptials, beaming for them and their wives, knowing their spouses had won the best husbands.

Many lunar cycles would pass before I finally counted myself worthy of such love. Still, my life would have turned out quite differently without the example of the Clarks. They taught me what to look for in a future husband and what it means to be cherished.

The journey to becoming a person is layered, some of our greatest secrets tucked away in a tightly sealed treasure chest at the bottom of the sea. Most spend their lives aware of the chest and the ramifications of opening it, unwilling to unearth the process of becoming whole. *I might drown*, they think. *It's not worth it*, they justify, sometimes drowning those around them as a result. When my therapist asked me to think of my happy place in one of our recent sessions, it came as no surprise that it was the seashore. I ended each session on the shore, surrounded by four people that rescued me from whatever I dug up that day, clasping hands and smiling, the wind blowing our hair every which way.

As I sit here brokenhearted, salty tears wetting my hands on the keyboard, I realize a close friend of the past several years was not on the seashore with me. Perhaps I took the relationship for granted, unwisely assuming that she would always be there. The taste of betrayal, however slight, burns like saltwater in an open wound, a lump ever-present in my throat. I do my best to choke it back.

"I wish I wasn't so sensitive," I tell my husband. "You balance me out," he replies with a smile. Images of our eleven-year union dance through my mind like an old black-and-white family reel, my waves constantly eroding his jagged edges, his rocks holding my steady flow. I know I will reach the shore again, but right now I struggle in deep waters, my nostrils just above the surface.

It was after a decade of marriage that I wondered if my husband, a calm and predictable river, was enough to match my sometimes unpredictable current. I caught sight of another man, seemingly walking in step with me in the sand. As I faced him, he mimed my every move. I raised my right arm; he shadowed it with his left. I moved my left leg; he was quick to pick up his right. He was as a triton commanding the water that surrounded him, and I felt drawn to his call. I stood in my husband's safe stream but constantly gazed at this other person.

As we looked into the water together, we had the same reflection. Everything around me became clouded, a sudden fog descending around my being. I looked down to see a serpent swimming around my ankles, and I abruptly crushed its head with my heel! *If you continue this way, you will drown, and so will your family*, a voice said. I ran desperately in the opposite direction, not glancing back to see what became of the other man. Years later, when I did finally meet this other man in person, I was unimpressed. This only drove me closer to my husband and confirmed how misleading the made-up world of social media can be.

My love of the shoreline drove me to exotic places around the world. The summer of 2007 found me in Puerto Rico, celebrating a girlfriend's thirtieth birthday. Mostly comprised of single women, our group squeezed every last ounce of carpe diem we could from the island: dancing to live salsa music at night, enjoying rum-tasting dinners, snorkeling on Icacos Island, and playing in the clear blue waves on the beaches. Spa day was my favorite. We were treated to hour-long, individual, beachside massages. Our masseuse, a heavy set, Hawaiian woman, worked miracles with her hands and a bottle of oil. She was strong and could have easily snapped me in two, gently and firmly working out the knots in my back. The movements of her hands were in sync with the sounds of the waves. If I could relive my greatest moment of relaxation, that would be it.

It was in 2003 that I encountered black (yes, black) sand for the first time. Formed by underground volcanoes, the Canary Islands off the northwestern coast of Africa are lush and tropical. A couple of months prior to landing on the largest island of Tenerife, my study abroad roommate in Spain, Samantha, handed me a colorful brochure and said, "I want to visit the Canary Islands. Want to come with me?" It wasn't the first or last time she would introduce me to a whole new experience. Tall with long, shapely legs and large doe-like brown eyes, bronze skin and chestnut colored hair, Samantha was the definition of sex appeal. In all our adventures together, European men seldom paid attention to the short, curly-haired, inexperienced cutie that accompanied her everywhere she went.

That spring semester abroad, the adventures were limitless, and my first debit card felt that way, too—plastic that had access to a never-ending portal of cash. Looking back, I did an impeccable job parsing out what I was given; it lasted the entire semester I was overseas. Our week on Tenerife had us riding trollies, taking part in a Jeep Safari adventure through a jungle, riding camels (after being directed to put on Arabic clothing over what we were wearing), and feeding a Saimiris.

On the beach, families made sculptures out of the black sand. It did not stick to every part of my body like the sand I had grown up with and brushed off much more easily. In my favorite picture from that trip, I am wearing a yellow tank top with bows at my shoulders and white-and-light blue striped capris, sitting on large, volcanic rocks with the rich blue and white waves of Tenerife crashing behind me. I didn't realize, at the time, that I was living some of the best days of my life. I packed some of the sand in a plastic water bottle and brought it back to the states with me, presenting it as a gift to my sister, Erin.

Anxious to share my experiences with family and friends, I often mailed postcards and sent regular e-mails. The internet cafes in Granada reeked of smoke, a grey cloud encircling you wherever you sat. I visited once a day, the Internet Explorer sign my ticket to connect with people back home and on my college campus. I have always been fond of writing.

Before I left Spain, tears streaming down my face, rolling my suitcase down the sidewalks of Granada with my backpack which had become a constant companion, I shared my photo journal with my Spanish family. Victoria, my señora, her husband Julio, their adult daughters Mari and Eva, and my roommate Samantha all enjoyed thumbing through my album. *No one has ever done anything like this*, they conceded. As they marveled at my semester highlights, I reminisced on all I would miss—huddling around a glass table covered by a cloth with a heater underneath every evening at 8 pm for supper, watching the news with extreme bias against the US, and simultaneously European fashion programs, walking home from the university, the smell of fresh strawberries and oranges lingering for blocks at a time, enjoying a *Shawarma* and orange pop (as I had come to call it in Iowa), sneaking candies out of my drawer in my room, and *Maria* cookies from the kitchen cupboards.

I would miss Victoria most of all, a woman who prided herself in caring for her home, family, and exchange students. My socks and underwear, which were carefully hung out the window on a line in between flats, have never been so white. She ironed them, every time, so each article of clothing was nice and crisp when I put it on. My favorite *postre*, so simple, was a dish of sliced strawberries left by the window for the afternoon, swimming in their natural juices when it came time to enjoy them after our meal. Yogurt was another sweet staple. She lived to serve us. As I remember her now almost twenty years later, I'm moved to thankful tears for her example. Some of her final words to me before I left, the highest you can bestow in the Spanish language, were *eres primor de niña* (you are a beautiful girl).

Something changes in your core when you move away from home and travel the world. The ability to see the world from a different perspective is a gift. When I came back to Brownsville before my senior year of college, my great uncle Ben called my bluff. "I see you've made your choice." Stumbling for words and backtracking, I assured him that I would never forget where I came from. He saw the truth: I had no desire to ever return.

Shortly after that, during a barbecue in my backyard with my family, I almost scoffed when my mother said, "Enjoying time with family during a barbecue is what life is all about."

"Maybe that's what it's about for you," I thought, "but I want so much more." Years passed before I realized she was right.

2020 has been a year of continual change and surprising developments. Each time we adjust to a new current, a more unpredictable one storms in, throwing off our balance and threatening to take us under.

I struggled to find my footing last year when all three children were finally in school, the youngest attending for half a day. Long had I fantasized about what would happen with that extra time. When I was living it, my days were far from glamorous.

I mourned what was and wondered who I was now that I wasn't raising children at home. Though the day-to-day monotony sometimes left me in a stupor, the time passed like vapor. Here temporarily, gone in three blinks, leaving me in a misty haze. I had just started coming out of the abyss when the Coronavirus struck.

Presently, masks and hand sanitizer are part of our routine wherever we go. *Masks required* signs adorn store windows and red tape on the ground shows which direction to travel down a particular aisle, or where to stand while appropriately socially distancing in line. If I didn't know any better, I'd think I was living the life of a character in a dystopian novel. When anyone coughs because of allergies or the like, everyone flinches and looks around, aghast that anyone with such a reflex would dare step foot outside their home.

Virtual schooling started in Brownsville, and I came close to having a minor breakdown, unable to be in three places (with my three children on individual devices) at once. The perfect COVID hurricane came crashing down on South Texas later than the rest of the state and country and wreaked havoc across our communities. Our people don't socially distance, not really. Greetings are typically a kiss on the cheek or a hug, at the very least. When Governor Abbott lifted the ban, we still had not experienced our first wave of the virus in the Rio Grande Valley. Precautions were not taken, and the firestorm of sickness and death erupted.

While we are finally on the other side of the peak, fear is rampant, and no one knows if and when we will go back to the lives we once knew. I echo what my six-year-old daughter, Cecily, said: "I just want everything to go back to normal."

South Padre Island proved a quaint escape for us when we needed it. We visited the week before school began and saw everyone else had the same idea—families huddling closely in clusters, couples jogging in their bathing suits on the sand, children feeding seagulls, and adults blasting music for all to hear.

The group to our immediate left brought six-packs of beer and kept adding them to their already full cooler. The blonde, middle-aged couple sloshed, hugging and kissing one another, occasionally making eye contact with me. *Isn't life ggggrrraaannnddddd?*

While I was annoyed that they were drunk in the late afternoon, I tried not to judge too harshly. Perhaps this was their way of coping, or not coping, with the present situation. Later they gallivanted in the shallow water, both their bodies telling stories through their tattoos. The woman smiled down at my four-year-old daughter, Felicity, and she smiled back. I concluded that we were all there for the same reason—to escape, to play, to feel good, to try to soak up as much normalcy sans masks as we possibly could.

Writing, in and of itself, has proved cathartic once again. I squeeze in time for my muse whenever I can, in between the sticky fingers of three tiny tyrants who now share our devices. My four-year-old has decided that virtual learning is not for her, dramatically hanging upside down on the swivel chair on her first day of school at 1:00 pm. The morning held such promise. I gave her a break today and taught her myself instead. What felt like my feet sinking and being stuck in the wet sand last week brought such joy this morning, her milk chocolate brown eyes and large smile beaming up at me.

As we ease into the fall season, I pray that it is kind. *Humanity needs a break, Lord. Please. I know this is election season. Have mercy on us and our land.* Visions of last Halloween, one of my favorite holidays, make me grin.

My father came, large speaker and copious amounts of candy in tow. Our neighborhood is one of *the* late October hotspots in Brownsville. Parents from all around, but mostly the nearby housing project, drop their children off in droves at the corner, slowly circling our blocks until it's time to pick them up. Our children passed out hundreds of sweets, recognizing classmates from their school just two minutes away. Our neighbors smiled and waved while we, typically quiet, blasted the likes of Michael Jackson and Queen on a giant speaker. My father is great for a party.

I don't know that we will host another extravagant fall activity this year. Our children's school sent a survey this week, asking if we will resume classes in person or continue virtually beginning September 29th. Suddenly, any question about the future feels like an assault. I have matured much in these last six months, evidenced by my grey wisdom lights that are showing up in all their glory. *We're here!* they announce. Now I understand what it means to literally not know what will happen from one day to the next. Truthfully, this is how things have always been, but we lived our lives differently before, foolishly thinking we could control them as much as we can command the sea to do as we please.

There's no place like fishing in the bay or the Arroyo for me. Water and I are not naturally friends. I have to take a small dose of Dramamine for seemingly simple activities—riding on an innertube around the lazy river at Schlitterbahn, for example. Any movement on boats is much the same, but it's worth it for me, when medicated, to feel the cool breeze and smell the salty air. *MMMmmmmmm.* My husband and I don't own a boat, but I've had some of the best experiences of my life when fishing with family and friends that do. "You get to have all the fun without all the hassle," he jokes.

It was in Arroyo City that I caught my first and only redfish, using a silver spoon lure as bait. The motor on my stepdad's boat had stalled and we were drifting for a good while. "Might as well try fishing here," he said.

What happened next is best described as an out-of-body experience. After a near perfect cast—a rarity—I imagined I *was* the fish and moved the line and bait accordingly. In the water, I saw something shiny, moving quickly and making a glorious sound. In an instant I felt a bite and pulled up as hard and as quickly as I could (also a timely miracle). The tip of my pole bent forward, my stepdad's eyes wide in amazement and my husband with a matching smile.

"Don't let it go!" LeRoy commanded. I followed the fish around the boat and over the motor, a back-and-forth tug of war I prayed I would win. I began reeling in the twenty-three-inch beauty, the men scrambling to get the net. The redfish was ours for the keeping! We caught nothing else that day, relying on another boat of men to help us get going again.

Like many who enjoy the sport, I have a small treasury of favorite fishing tales. The first time we went out with Chris and Meagan Rasco, we were goners, simultaneously falling in love with them and catching trout in the bay. Altogether we caught about twenty keepers that day, our loot so large it tore the net, another biblical reference.

I asked endless questions on that trip, finding a patient teacher in Chris. He never flinched when I carefully cast my line, even when it got caught in inconvenient places. "We need to go where the fish are," he'd say as the anchor pulled up, a small buzz under our feet. He called my husband and me "naturals." We believed him.

On one of our excursions, we were convinced Chris had landed a big one. It became increasingly difficult to lure in. It was a sea turtle! After he carefully removed the hook, we took quick pictures with it, and then we released it back where it belonged. I beamed that day, having had a close encounter with nature. It was incredible.

I imagine that my love affair with the sea will be lifelong. My family and I are presently planning one last visit before temperatures drop and heavy rain falls, marking the beginning of autumn in South Texas. This is the time of year that my limbs begin breaking out; my PLC yearns for sun and saltwater as the best treatment. My husband and children will play in the water while I sit and exfoliate my arms and legs and rinse them in the ocean. It's ironic that I spent much of my life trying to hide my skin condition, and the only way it improves is by being exposed to natural elements. The coast continues to be my healing place.

While I do not know what comes next, I know I will continue to follow the current. The One who created both the sea and me promises that *"living water will flow from [my] heart"* in any season I find myself in. Thus, I continue sitting by the water, my toes deep in the sand and vision expectant on the horizon.

G.G. (Giana Gallardo) Hesterberg was born and raised in Brownsville, Texas. She studied at Central College in Pella, Iowa, and received a Bachelor's degree in Elementary Education in 2004. She published her first book, Stories by the Seashore, *in March of 2019. Her second book,* Music, Music, You Can Too!, *a nonfiction children's book, was released in July 2020. Hesterberg is currently a graduate student. She lives in South Texas with her husband, three children, and a dog.*

POEMS I WROTE TO THE BEACH

Salome Solomon

The Mitochondrial Eve

A shadow of permission
With helix strands as fingers
You'd think the nucleus that holds us
Would be enough to keep us

Yet here we are
Blistering fists of self-righteousness
On the throat of equality
Barking like dogs
At the new dawn
Of millennial tribalism

San Juan Island

Whales must loathe diving for air
Dispatching ripples of unease
The crash of valor
To the applause of a fishbowl

Sleepy eyes
Encased in the crust of friends
He turns sideways

And for a moment
Belly up, his skin a trampoline
Flinging elastic dots of infrared white
I am also tempted to bounce with the light

You held my arm
Gripping the marvel of a god's creation
That was him and me and us
And the beach we were on

The cool dapple of sunshine
The gritty remains of ocean's fury
I had forgotten that we had forgotten
That no god would create such an energy
Just to marvel amidst its destruction
And I don't know who decided
That we as a race
Should.

Useless Bay

there was a moment I thought I saw shore

my saltwater gums a well of maple saliva
i could swear there was land dry enough to make candy on

my scars always fade   into
pleasant splatters and tiger stripes

they had darkened that morning
cells turned over to the push of August's sun

i share seventy percent raw material
with the cerulean hem of the Puget Sound
was I truly born to straddle this edge
as silk thread on a holiday gown –

one-part decorative one-part imperative
?.

i pose you for pictures that yearn for a space
i feel too small to fill.

My Generation Doesn't Know
How to Date

Slow clap
To the Ferris wheel
With its seats full of props
And a toast
To the internet
Our erratic foster mother

Love comes in all shapes
Sizes and intentions -
And vanity is the newest
contestant in the game

Unloading My Traumas
at Edmonds Beach

Here, it's okay to whither
Drooling skies shake their knees
The ocean says its fine to weep
She does it all the time
And I still love Her don't I?

When I return to that tepid valley
Growing lush with my loves and failures
I can say that the salt tracks on my cheeks
Were hand painted by god
And I can interpret that art however I like

❦

'Poems I Wrote to the Beach' is a small collection of poems I wrote when I felt too small and the world felt too large. This is a myth that can deafen you if you let it. I'm grateful to be alongside the talented writers of Women Write Now *to share how I felt about this myth.*

Salome Solomon, or Homeland Obscurity, began with a fiercely private exploration of the evolution of culture, self, and home through varied mediums. A story teller from childhood, Homeland Obscurity illustrates her taste for society, and curiosity for the people who create it by operating a multifaceted office. One part poetry, one part fine paintings, one part photography, Homeland Obscurity uses her wit and speculative eye to portray her musings on who we are today.

Where is Home?

Armin Parhami

"You think you took my house?" I asked the mortgage attorney, tears running down my cheeks.

She looked at me and sneered. "Were you not there? We just bought your house at auction. It's not yours anymore."

I sternly looked into her eyes and replied, "No. You did not because I have not allowed you to."

———

I had woken up to multiple rings of my doorbell, followed by harsh banging at the door. Who could it be this early in the morning in my peaceful, well-to-do neighborhood?

I quickly put on my robe and went downstairs so the children would not wake up. Two sheriffs were at the door.

"How may I help you?" They handed me some papers. Through disbelief, I read the words NOTICE OF DEFAULT.

Our house was going to be foreclosed soon.

All four of my kids came down to see what the noise was all about. "Oh, it was just the sheriff with some paperwork he needed to deliver," I said casually.

My heart was pounding and my head was spinning. What am I going to do? Where will I live with the kids? My youngest was three years old, and my oldest fourteen.

The bank refused to speak to me about my loan and its possible modification, as I was on the mortgage but not on the note. The bank would only communicate with my husband, who was MIA.

I had not worked for seventeen years and didn't even know how to create an email account. I had trusted my husband with all of our finances and occupied myself with raising my children, my greatest joy and passion in life.

Since my husband had disappeared and suddenly "lost his job," no money was coming in. My divorce attorney suggested a real estate attorney to help me, but I later learned that the real estate attorney had been recruited and paid by my ex to speed up the foreclosure.

I contacted my state officials, many attorneys, and explored every possible avenue to speak to my lender, frantic yet steady in my efforts.

They all said that nothing could be done. "Just let the house go," they all told me.

Where would I go with my four kids? The more I thought about it and the more I persisted in my efforts, the more the gloomy reality set in: a foreclosure was inevitable.

But then, a small miracle. God stepped in—at least temporarily. President Obama put the whole foreclosure process for homeowners on hold for a year and a half. Phew! This will give me some time to figure things out, I thought.

Alas, fast forward a year and a half: The sheriff was back, with a foreclosure notice and an auction date in hand. An auction? Suddenly, I felt a surge of hope. Maybe I can ask a friend to come and put a low bid on the house and buy it, and then I would rent it from them.

I started contacting my well-off friends.

It's funny how our friends are plentiful in our times of abundance, but in our times of need, they are often nowhere to be found. Finally, a friend of a friend who lived in Canada decided to come to the auction to buy the house.

In the meantime, I contacted my ex's relatives, begging them to ask my ex to cooperate and talk to the bank for loan modification purposes. They convinced him, and for a short period of time he talked to the bank and sent the required documents. The bank pretended that it was working with us and that the auction and foreclosure were put on hold.

On the day of the supposedly postponed auction, I got a strange feeling in the pit of my stomach—a voice telling me to go to the auction anyway. To my disbelief, I went and saw my house going up for sale and my lender buying it.

"You think you took my house?" I asked the mortgage attorney, tears running down my cheeks.

She looked at me and sneered. "Were you not there? We just bought your house at auction. It's not yours anymore."

I sternly looked into her eyes and replied, "No. You did not because I have not allowed you to."

I had no lawyer, no money, and no connections I could rely on. However, by attending the auction, I now knew the fate that awaited me instead of being hit with a surprise eviction notice.

I called legal aid and asked for help to file an emergency petition on my behalf. If legal aid would guide me in the correct direction, I promised to do most of the work—which I did.

I overturned the foreclosure in 24 hours.

━━━━━━

Armin Parhami is a single mother of four who believes in and creates miracles! Despite many obstacles in her life, she has managed to raise four amazing and successful children all on her own. She came to the United States (to the frigid state of North Dakota) as a child from Iran to escape religious persecution. She received her Bachelor of Arts from the University of Minnesota and currently lives in Northern Virginia with her 16-year-old daughter.

At the start of the pandemic, she, with the help of her children, created a successful weekly, interactive, and global online talk series with effective and highly qualified speakers to address the critical current needs of humanity and the solutions for those needs. The series is still ongoing and attracts people from all over the world who want to join in these important discourses.

Armin wants to give hope to all those single moms who are pulling a double shift 24/7 and raising their children alone, ladies feeling inadequate and thinking that one needs a "perfect" family to raise wonderful and successful children. She also loves to create miracles in the kitchen for her loved ones!

TEENAGE MOM

Liselle Powder

I write this story to support anyone who is experiencing an unexpected or unplanned pregnancy. My story is meant to encourage and build family closeness and togetherness after a very touching dilemma that I went through. I have learned and grown from this challenge, and I hope you, the reader, will learn and grow from this story that I have written.

"Mummy, I am pregnant." Those words hit me like lightning. I felt like all my pores and every living organ in my body leaped with every beat of my heart. On December 28th, 2017, my world fell apart. What transpired that day will be a lasting memory in my mind.

Sometimes tragedies will either make you or break you. If you want to survive and live for another day, it's a winning situation all the way.

—

As a single mother with two daughters, I have had to work extra-hard to stay on top of things to keep my family happy, healthy, and safe. After months of staying in hotels and motels, sleeping wherever our heads could rest, my daughters and I were traumatized and exhausted. I knew our living situation was unhealthy for us in so many ways.

In particular, I worried about my youngest daughter Stephanie. She was young, bright, beautiful and full of life, but also on the quiet side. She loved life, parties, and family get-togethers, but because of her quiet nature, I wasn't always aware of what was going on with her. I certainly didn't know that what lay ahead was hidden in the depths of her soul waiting to be awakened.

Stephanie tended to be in her own world and keep to herself. She had a few friends at school, but there was one character that stood out from the crowd. His name was Bryan. Stephanie loved Bryan with a love that will never die, very much like the kind of love you might see in fairy tale movies.

As someone who had been married and divorced twice, I was always cautious with my girls. Not that they were headed down the same path I took, but I relied on my mother's instincts to help me stay in touch with what was going on with them. At least, I tried to.

Stephanie introduced me to Bryan, who was humble and soft spoken with a voice that said *I am a decent guy*, a voice that said *I was raised with respect and manners*. I guess he must have felt a bit intimidated by me as I was her mother. Nevertheless, I welcomed him with open arms.

Stephanie would go out after school with Bryan, and I would let her know not to be out too late as we were staying at a hotel. As time went by, my daughter would extend her late nights till the morning hours.

I started to question myself. What have I done? How am I going to fix this? I felt the urgency in my heart to put a stop to everything. I felt I was losing myself. I felt I was not in control anymore. I became fearful: Am I really the mother in this situation?

At one point, I asked my eldest daughter Bridget what to do. I lost control of everything that I represented, being the protector, mother, advisor, you name it. How could I get back to being the head of the household?

I tried talking to Stephanie about what she was doing and how I believed it was wrong. She kept telling me that everything was okay. But I knew deep down inside it wasn't.

I felt lost and hopeless. Who could I reach out to? Bridget was dealing with her own struggles with her job and all the stuff a young adult has to face. The troubles both my girls were going through sent me back to memory lane.

I saw the boyfriends, the wanting to belong, the sleepless nights, the running from door to door, the confrontations, the break ups and the make ups. I saw it all. I cried out NO! The tears flowed as I tried to get a grip on reality. I looked in the mirror with the tears gushing out like a dam bursting its banks. Through the tears, I said to myself that I have to take back my household. I have to make a stand. I have to change some rules.

The first rule was no more late nights. Around this time, a lottery system to get one of the beautiful apartments in the Suffolk County area was taking place. Despite what I was facing with my daughter, I had to push forward, believing in and telling myself, "I have to find a place to live."

I called the company and got all the information needed to get that apartment. I filled out the application, sent it in, and waited. I was determined to keep my family together.

After a while, I saw the change in Stephanie. She became withdrawn, and we had fewer conversations. Even though she was adhering to the rules, I knew something was wrong. I wanted her to talk to me. Tell me where it hurts. What can I do to ease the pain? All my motherly knowledge was thrown out the door and I felt helpless again. I felt like I was losing my mind and I just have to say I gave up.

On April 7th, 2017, I got a letter in the mail, letting me know that my name was picked from the stack of applications for the apartments. I was so elated that I screamed at the top of my voice. HALLELUJAH! HALLELUJAH!

My life was taking a turn for the better. No more running, no more back and forth, no more hotels and motels. Both my girls were thrilled with the news, even Stephanie, despite the fact she was rapidly pulling away from me. My worry for her increased, yet the show must go on—I had to get ready for our new home.

I started getting my documents together to be processed and making sure everything was up- to-date. While preparing for the interview, which would involve the three of us, I had to beg my youngest to be there. It was as if she no longer cared about this fantastic opportunity.

I lost the battle to keep Stephanie in order. She slept out most of the time and her attitude became aggressive, so aggressive that when we came into contact, we screamed at each other. Where was my daughter that I birthed? The sweet innocent girl who called me Mom? The little girl whose hair I would comb and adorn with pretty bubbles. Where was my daughter? The little girl who ate ice cream and lolly sticks. Where was my daughter? The daughter I packed lunch and fruit for, the daughter I hugged and sang rock-a-bye-baby to.

My daughter was growing up and she didn't need me anymore—this was the sad truth I faced.

After all my documents were submitted and the interview was successful, I was told I could move in. This was the news I was waiting to hear, and my heart leaped for joy. I was so emotional I couldn't contain myself. The tears of joy flowed.

On August 3rd I moved into my brand-new apartment, and being the first occupant was a blessing. However, this was when everything took a turn for the worst with my daughter.

The night we moved in, Stephanie was out of control. She told me I needed to get a life and stop meddling in hers. She said she was of age to make her decisions; no one could tell her what to do. Shouting and screaming at me.

I felt so hurt and discouraged. I wanted to run far away, and the thought came to end my life. I just ran out of the apartment and sat down in the car park crying so loud. Why me? Why me? The beating of my heart felt like drums in a parade, and I could practically count the beats that rocked my soul. My eldest tried consoling me. I got great support from her. But I didn't see Stephanie for a long time after that.

After I moved in everything, I had to heal and try to move forward. I missed Stephanie so much. She slept over at Bryan's house and did everything from there like going to school and going to work. I couldn't believe that the boy's family would encourage such behavior. It made me so mad, but I had to leave it alone and try to keep calm.

I started to feel very sick with nausea and wanting to throw up. I went to see the doctor and I was diagnosed with high blood pressure. I couldn't believe it. Never would I have thought that this dreadful disease would catch up with me. My friends advised me to take it easy and to leave Stephanie to herself, but I couldn't do it. I pushed and pushed to talk to her until she stopped communicating. Which was the last thing I wanted to happen.

After a while, things started to get better (but not quite) between Stephanie and me. So much was lost in communication, so many things were said, and I had to take it easy because of my blood pressure. Stephanie would come by and spend time, but I told her she had to make a choice to either stay with me or stay with the boy's family. She made up her mind to stay with the boy's family.

As time went by, Stephanie would call to get stuff to eat and I would let her come over. At one point, I watched her and said to myself, "Wow, she is surely eating up a storm." I didn't think anything of it, just looked at it as her being hungry.

One day she came over to eat and, in a few seconds, she was vomiting all over the floor. Bridget ran into the kitchen to find out what was going on. I was so speechless that my mouth remained wide open.

Then Stephanie said, "I am so sorry. Must've been something bad I ate earlier." I felt the tug in my stomach. I watched Bridget and then Stephanie, speechless, confused, and with so many mixed emotions. What to say? Nothing, not a word.

The apartment was so silent, that a pin, the shuffling of feet, or anything that moved, echoed. I left immediately and went outside. Then words spilled from my mouth. I was babbling like I went into another world of madness, talking to myself, questioning myself, accusing myself. Even laughing to myself.

Have I gone mad regarding the incident that just transpired in the apartment? No. I am okay. I am Mother. I am me. Get yourself together, I said to myself. I can do this, and I took some deep breaths. I am ready to face my fear.

I walked back to the apartment and Stephanie was crying. "Mummy, I am so sorry. Mummy, please forgive me. Mummy, I am pregnant." What to do as a mother hearing those words? All I could do was cry and hug her. Bridget came over and hugged us, too.

While all the hugging was going on, my mind raced. The thoughts in my head battled each other. Positive outcomes and negative outcomes, and my eyes opened wide as reality kicked in.

Where is this money coming from to support this baby? Did the boy's parents know? Another mouth to feed, Pampers, milk, doctor visits. All the questions were doing double Dutch in my mind.

I felt another rush to my head—my blood pressure. So caught up in all the drama that I forgot to take my pills. I had to take it easy. I had to compose myself. I released my daughter, and the big question was, "How far along are you?"

She answered, "Five months."

I was in shock. As I looked back, I remembered all those outbursts, but I never saw a thing. How could I have missed it? Are my motherly instincts failing me again? My daughter is very slim and at nineteen years old, her body made it difficult to see any bump. Most of the time the clothes she wore were oversized. Bridget was still in shock, and the only thing for us to do was try to cope with the new addition.

I asked my daughter if Bryan's parents knew. She said no, and I said they needed to be told. Bryan knew about the pregnancy, and he had been going to the doctor with her. Eventually I said,

"Everything will be okay." But deep inside anger rose. How can I say it's going to be okay? I should make her pay for her disobedience. Why should I help her? This is not my problem, it's hers.

The more I tried to dismiss the negatives and cling to the positives, it was not working. Somehow the bitterness and the anger inside got the better part of me. I started to reject her. I couldn't face her, which caused her to spend more time with Bryan's family. Many times, I thought of hurting myself or running away and never turning back.

The mere thought that my daughter was pregnant hurt every part of my body inside out. I looked back to when I had been pregnant, and the emotional turmoil I had been in. I asked myself, am I going to see the same thing unfold before me? I looked up to the heavens and cried out to God. Help me! I can't do this on my own. I need you to help me, please.

Weeks passed by. Bridget was more out than in. She found comfort with her friends, and they helped her deal with the situation.

One day, Stephanie asked to see me, and I was more than ready to see her. I welcomed my daughter with open arms, forgetting myself for once and dealing with the situation at hand. In such a short space of time, Stephanie's belly was now showing. I had to comfort her and make sure that everything was fine with her and the baby.

I went the extra mile, making sure that food was in the house, providing taxi fare for her to go to the doctor, and buying clothes for her and the baby. I kept thinking, "I'm going to be a grandma, soon!"

I made sure she was comfortable in her bed, changing sheets when they needed changing, combing her hair, rubbing her tummy when the pressure was too much, rubbing her feet and making sure they were elevated, and cooking her favorite meals.

Stephanie had to quit her jobs, and the school made it possible for her to get tutored at home before the baby was due. Different tutors came about three times a week. My daughter wanted to give up because the baby's pressure in the pelvic area was causing some discomfort for her. I told her to be strong, just as I kept telling myself to be strong. Praying for my sanity and asking God to give me the strength to survive as at times I felt weak and hopeless, but I had to be strong for her.

After doing all that, I was back on memory lane. I remember being so sick with my pregnancies and coping with limited help. I had to do almost everything for myself, and if I was sick, I would lie in bed wanting the time to fly by. I lost count of the number of times I vomited. The emptiness in my stomach mimicked how I felt emotionally most of the time.

I had to save my daughter from going through the same depression I suffered. Every time I went out and saw babies with their mothers, my heart would be joyful. Soon, it'll be me who will be a grandmother. Yes, it'll be me up some nights with the baby. Yes, it'll be me helping out with making the formula. Yes, it'll be me comforting mother and child. Yes, it'll be me.

Once, we had a false alarm. My daughter had to be rushed to the hospital because she felt the baby pushing, but it was the baby positioning itself to make its way into the world. I told her that a few times, but her pain was so bad we called the ambulance just to be safe. All the way there, she screamed in pain. "Mummy! Mummy!"

I said, "I am right here, baby. I am right here."

I did wonder, though, if I should leave her at the hospital to face her situation alone, or if I should work harder to put aside the hurts from her disrespect towards me. It was now or never. But looking at her face I chose to hold her. I chose to be there for her. I chose to be supportive. I am her mother.

I prayed for her, held her hands tight, let her know it was going to be okay, and that I was there for her. The contractions were coming fast. She was in a lot of pain and I told her to do her breathing exercises, till at one point in time I found myself breathing with her as though I was the one having the baby.

We reached the hospital and the nurses wasted no time checking her. There was no dilation, just tremendous pressure. The doctor came in to check and still no dilation. My baby, my tender flower, was crying and saying, "Mummy, I am so sorry. Please forgive me, please forgive me, please forgive me. Please!"

I looked up as the tears streamed down my face, and I felt as if God was telling me to do the right thing. I said, "I forgive you and I love you. We will get through this together." Mother and daughter bonded, as we held each other crying, not letting go of each other.

The nurses scheduled my daughter for some tests. I was concerned. After the tests, the doctors and nurses came in and told my daughter that they saw a lot of fluid in the sac and that this could be dangerous. I kept on praying and asking God to forgive me and to forgive my daughter. I knew I had to forgive myself. I called my friends to pray and I told Bridget to pray also.

Stephanie was in contact with Bryan's family, and I spoke to them over the phone for the first time. I was not upset, not because I could've been, but because it was a time of healing for both families, which I accepted.

After two days in the hospital and no progress, the nurses had to induce labor. Seeing my daughter lying there with all the tubes hooked up and the machines beeping was very sad and emotional for me. There was not much talking between my daughter and myself, as she was in a lot of pain. But the prayers from family and friends were uplifting and encouraging. A few friends and co-workers came to visit us and brought items for the baby.

Their generosity reminded me of the beautiful baby shower that my co-workers held for me and my daughter—so much to be thankful for. There was no change after inducing labor twice, and the decision was made to do a C-section.

The nurses got my daughter ready to go to the operating room. I had to put on scrubs and some funny-looking shoes and gloves. Bryan came by, but he couldn't come to the operating room.

My mind was in deep thought and prayer. I sat down and looked over as they gave my daughter the injection to numb her body. My daughter's eyes were open as the procedure began. The doctors had to move their hands very fast because the baby was in danger from being in the sac with the extra fluids.

I heard an uproar of voices and then cheers. The baby was out. The nurses hurriedly made sure she was alive and cut the umbilical cord. They wiped her up and would you believe she was sleeping all this time? Not a sound was heard from her. But she was alive and well. I counted her fingers and toes, and a smile of happiness filled my face.

Stephanie looked up, and I told her she had a beautiful girl. Stephanie chose the name Sabrina. The doctors and nurses were busy cleaning up the room, so I gave them their space. Eventually Stephanie and the baby were wheeled to a spacious room, very nice and quiet.

I had to show Stephanie how to breast feed, although the nurses came in every so often and checked to make sure all was well. I had to help my daughter off the bed to use the bathroom; she was like a helpless child. Despite the pain from the C-section, my daughter had to walk again, so I made her pace the hallways up and down. I got the time off from work to be there for Stephanie in the hospital. I was so glad to be there for her as the feeling of love and togetherness unfolded.

Sabrina slept most of the time. Only when she was hungry would she open her mouth for nourishment. As Stephanie and the baby rested, I looked at both of them and smiled to myself, saying everything is going to be alright.

Bryan came by after school, and I finally met his parents face-to-face. I was cordial. I spoke about what transpired but without all the anger I'd been feeling months earlier. It was me changing for the better. No longer was I upset, no more bitterness, no more hate. We are now a simple family trying to fit the pieces together, searching for ways to come up with the best solutions to move forward.

I stood there watching them interact with Stephanie and the baby. After they left, I asked my daughter how she felt. Even though the pain was bad, she felt good and thanked me so much for not giving up on her.

My daughter was discharged, and I felt happy, as everything was perfect. We were going home. I will always be mother, grandmother, friend, sister, and I have made the choice to listen and be supportive always. YES!

Blessings.

———◆———

Liselle Powder was born on the small Caribbean island of Trinidad and Tobago. Born to Edwina Warner (deceased) and Bindley Powder, she is the last of six siblings. She is divorced with two daughters and a granddaughter.

Having immigrated to the U.S. in 2014, Liselle decided to write poetry about her experiences coming to America. She met Edna White, an author, and the rest is history. Liselle wrote a story for Edna's book No Sweet Meat! Tell Me the Truth *and contributes to the school newspaper where she works. She also writes for Edna's magazine called* Speak Magazine. *Liselle's short stories were included in issues of* Speak Magazine *in 2020 and 2021.*

Liselle is also an artist and hopes to have her first art show in the near future. She has sold some of her art work.

Liselle's first poetry book, Still Overcoming, *was published in 2020. Her first poetry reading received excellent reviews, so she is now working on a second book of poetry. She has come a long way and strives to be one of the best poets and artists the world has yet to see.*